the

book

of

GAMES

for

children's

ministry

Loveland, Colorado

Group's R.E.A.L. Guarantee to you:

Every Group resource incorporates our R.E.A.L. approach to ministry—a unique philosophy that results in long-term retention and life transformation. It's ministry that's:

**This is EARL.
He's R.E.A.L.
mixed up.
(Get it?)**

Relational
Because student-to-student interaction enhances learning and builds Christian friendships.

Experiential
Because what students experience sticks with them up to 9 times longer than what they simply hear or read.

Applicable
Because the aim of Christian education is to be both hearers and doers of the Word.

Learner-based
Because students learn more and retain it longer when the process is designed according to how they learn best.

The Humongous Book of Games for Children's Ministry

Copyright © 2002 Group Publishing, Inc.

Visit our Web site: **www.group.com**

CREDITS
Editor: Cindy S. Hansen
Acquisitions Editor: Karl Leuthauser
Chief Creative Officer: Joani Schultz
Copy Editor: Betty Taylor
Art Directors: Andrea L. Boven and Jean Bruns
Designer: Andrea L. Boven/Boven Design Studio, Inc.
Computer Graphic Artists: Pat Miller and Tracy K. Donaldson
Illustrator: Shelley Dieterichs
Cover Art Director: Bambi Morehead
Cover Illustrator: Amy Wummer
Production Manager: DeAnne Lear

Library of Congress Cataloging-in-Publication Data
The humongous book of games for children's ministry/ [from the editors of] Group Publishing.
ISBN 0-7644-2355-X
15 14 13 12 11 10 9 8 7 6   12 11 10 09 08 07 06 05

Printed in the United States of America.

Contents

☆ ☆ ☆ ☆ ☆ EARLY ELEMENTARY GAMES ☆ ☆ ☆ ☆ ☆

☆ ☆ ☆ ☆ ☆
UPPER ELEMENTARY GAMES
☆ ☆ ☆ ☆ ☆

Introduction

Playing games. Ask the children in your ministry what they love about your ministry and you're almost guaranteed to hear, "Playing games." Play is an integral part of childhood. And it's an integral part of ministry, too. As children play, they're having fun while they're learning. Games teach children about patience, respect, cooperation, and encouragement.

Games involve everyone, and they're a powerful tool for making a point. If you wanted to teach children about David and Goliath, you could sit them down in rows, tell them the story, and have them color in a picture of David. Or...you could have them play Human Slingshots (page 110), in which they link arms to make "slings" and launch paper "rocks" at a nine-foot-high target. Which do you think children will remember? Which will they enjoy?

The Humongous Book of Games for Children's Ministry has hundreds of games that connect with many different topics and hundreds of different Scriptures. The book is divided into three main sections: "Preschool Games," "Lower Elementary Games," and

"Upper Elementary Games." If you're teaching your preschoolers about a topic and you need an opening game, just look at the table of contents to find the game that fits the point you're making. If you want your fifth-graders to understand a certain Scripture passage, just turn to the "Scripture Index" in the back to find the game that brings the passage to life. If your second-graders need a change of pace, turn to the "Energy Level Index" to find a high-energy game to liven things up.

The Humongous Book of Games for Children's Ministry probably has all the games you'll need. Have fun laughing, learning, and playing!

Preschool Games

Jesus said, "Let the little children come to me" (Luke 18:16). You can see why! Little children are awesome. They *know* Jesus loves them. The light of Jesus' love shines through their eyes.

Use the games in this section to keep the light burning bright in the eyes of children in preschool and kindergarten. These fun games are noncompetitive, so the little ones can play to their heart's content and not feel sad about "losing out" on the action. The discussion questions within each game help preschoolers connect to real-life issues such as making new friends, learning how to show love to others, and practicing how to obey Jesus' commands.

Give a Little, Take a Lot

Topic: Abraham

Scripture: Genesis 13

Game Overview: Kids will race to divide into groups according to categories.

☆ ☆ ☆ ☆ ☆

Supplies: Bible, chair, stopwatch

Preparation: Place a chair at the center front of the class.

Open your Bible to Genesis 13, and tell the kids about how Abraham and his nephew Lot divided the land. Lot got to choose first! Say: **I'll be Lot** (stand at one side of the chair), **and you'll be Abraham.** Choose someone to be Abraham, and have the child stand on the other side of the chair. **You're the land!** Point to the children. **If you're part of my land, come sit in front of me. If you're part of Abraham's land, sit in front of our friend, Abraham.**

I, Lot, will take everyone who's wearing stripes. Abraham will say: "I'll take everyone who's *not* wearing stripes." Let Abraham repeat after you.

Encourage children to move to the proper sides of the room. Time them to see how quickly they divide. Then choose another Abraham, and decide on a different feature by which to divide the class, such as tennis shoes/no tennis shoes, shoelaces/no shoelaces, buttons/no buttons, wearing red/not wearing red. Time each division to see how quickly kids can do it.

☆ ☆ ☆ ☆ ☆

At the end of the game, discuss the following questions:

· **What was it like to be Abraham and get what Lot didn't?**

· **When have you been the last one to get to pick something?**

Say: **God was in control all of Abraham's life. Even though Lot picked what he wanted first, God blessed Abraham with riches, long life, and lots of family to love him!**

Leader Tip

After kids play for a while with you as Lot, let them take turns being both Lot and Abraham. You could also divide the class into two groups, with each group having a Lot and an Abraham. That way "lots" of kids can be Lots and Abrahams in a shorter amount of time!

Abraham's Servant Relay

Topic: Abraham

Scripture: Genesis 24

Game Overview: Kids will race against time to complete a relay race.

☆ ☆ ☆ ☆ ☆

Supplies: Bible, stopwatch

Preparation: Clear the playing area.

O pen your Bible to Genesis 24, and tell kids about Abraham sending his servant on a long trip to find a wife for his son Isaac. Say: **Let's play a game and pretend we're traveling with Abraham's servant.**

Have kids form two equal teams and stand in two lines on one side of your playing area. Say: **To start our game, the first person in each line will travel across the room and back, then tag the hand of the next person who'll travel the same way. The catch is, you have to move the way I tell you to. Every now and then, I'll call out a different way for you to move.**

Practice the modes of traveling that you'll call out:

• **Ride a camel** (walk on all fours).

• **Kneel in prayer** (walk on knees).

• **Dance and clap with joy** (dance any way they want as they clap).

• **Bow down to God** (walk or run in a bowed-down position, with fingertips touching the ground).

After practicing, have kids run the relay as you randomly call out the modes of traveling. Time how long the relay takes to complete. Then have kids run the relay several times, trying to beat their best time.

☆ ☆ ☆ ☆ ☆

At the end of the relay, discuss the following questions:

• **Which part of this relay was difficult for you? easy?**

• **How do you think Abraham's servant traveled?**

Say: **God was with Abraham's servant during his long, hard trip. God helped the servant find a wife who loved Isaac forever!**

Back-sket Ball

Topic: Cooperation

Scripture: 1 Corinthians 3:9a

Game Overview: Kids will work together to crab walk and carry balls to baskets.

☆　☆　☆　☆　☆

Supplies: Two different types of balls, two laundry baskets, stopwatch

Preparation: Gather two different types of balls such as large Nerf balls, beach balls, or inflated Mylar balloons. You'll need eight to ten of each type of ball. Place the laundry baskets about fifteen feet apart.

Form two groups, and have each group stand by a laundry basket. Then assign a type of ball to each group.

Say: **When I say "Go," work as a team to collect your balls and put them in your laundry basket. It would be pretty easy if you could just run around the room and collect them, but instead you can move only by doing the crab walk!** Ask a child to demonstrate. **You can use your hands to pick up a ball, but then you have to balance it on your tummy or hold it between your knees as you crab walk the ball to your basket. Work together with your team and cheer one another on. Ready? Go!**

Tell kids that when they've finished collecting their team's balls, they can help the other team collect its balls, too. Time kids to see how long it takes for both teams to collect their balls. Play again, and have kids try to beat that time.

☆　☆　☆　☆　☆

At the end of the game, discuss the following questions:

• **How did you work as a team to get all your balls in your basket?**

• **How did you work with the other team and help its members get their balls in their basket?**

Read 1 Corinthians 3:9a, and then say: **We are God's fellow workers! Just as you worked together as a team in the game, we all work together with God. Let's work together to tell everyone how much God loves each of us!**

Balancing Act

Topic: Cooperation

Scripture: 2 Corinthians 7:4

Game Overview: Kids will encourage each other as they work with partners to balance a ball on a seesaw.

☆ ☆ ☆ ☆ ☆

Supplies: Round containers, cardboard, balls

Preparation: For every two children, you'll need a round container such as an empty oatmeal box, a tennis ball, and a piece of cardboard that's as wide as the container and about two feet long.

Have kids form pairs, and give each pair a round container, a ball, and a piece of cardboard. Show kids how to lay the container on its side, position the cardboard on top of it, then try to balance the ball on top of the cardboard while gently tipping the cardboard back and forth like a seesaw.

Before pairs try the balancing act themselves, read 2 Corinthians 7:4 and say: **You're an awesome group of kids, and I *know* you'll be able to work together to balance your ball. I have great confidence in you! Encourage each other as you work.** Say, **"Good job" or "I know you can do it!"**

Have pairs work together, encouraging each other as they balance their balls on the cardboard.

Leader Tip

For more fun, blow a whistle every thirty seconds, and have children switch partners.

☆ ☆ ☆ ☆ ☆

At the end of the game, discuss the following questions:

· **How did you work together with your partner to balance the ball?**

· **Who else can you help today?**

· **What encouraging words can you say?**

Say: **No matter who we help during the day, let's remember to say good things to each other. We feel happy when others help and encourage us, and we make others feel happy when we help and encourage them.**

Belly Bonanza

Topic: Cooperation

Scripture: Ecclesiastes 4:9-10a

Game Overview: Kids will help partners retrieve special treats.

☆ ☆ ☆ ☆ ☆

Supplies: Bible, pillows (one for each pair of kids), candy or fruit snacks (four bags)

Preparation: Open the bags of treats, and place one bag on a table at each corner of the room.

Help kids find partners, and give each pair a pillow. Say: **Before we play this game, let's practice what you'll be doing. Stand, face your partner, and put your pillow between your bellies. You'll have to lean together to hold it in place. Try walking with your partner so the pillow doesn't fall. Don't use your hands to hold the pillow, but you may use your hands to hug each other, so you stay close!** Let kids practice for a while.

After kids have practiced, say: **I've put a bag of treats in each corner.** Point to each corner. **When I say "Go," you and your partner have two minutes to get a treat from each bag. If you drop your pillow, stop, pick it up, and put it back between your bellies before you continue. Ready? Go!**

☆ ☆ ☆ ☆ ☆

At the end of the game, have kids sit with their partners and hold their candies. Discuss the following question:

• **How did you help each other get your treats?**

Read Ecclesiastes 4:9-10a; then ask:

• **What does the Bible tell us about friends helping each other?**

Say: **Friends can help each other, and they get a good treat for their work! Let's eat our treats and tell our partners, "Thanks for the help!"**

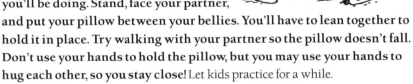

Leader Tip

Make the game more challenging for older kids. Have one partner close his or her eyes while the other partner tells him or her where to go. No hands allowed. You could also place the open bags of candy on the floor in the four corners rather than on tables.

Animal Action

Topic: Creation

Scripture: Genesis 2:19-20

Game Overview: Kids will enjoy becoming Adam's new zoo.

☆ ☆ ☆ ☆ ☆

Supplies: Bible

Preparation: To help you think quickly on your feet, write out a list of "birds of the air" such as eagles, robins, crows, sparrows, and geese. Make another list of "beasts of the field" such as cows, lions, dogs, cats, horses, and monkeys.

Seat children in a group so that all of them can see you. Open your Bible to Genesis 2:19-20, and read the verses out loud.

Say: **Let's pretend that I'm Adam and you're the birds of the air and beasts of the field that God made. God has given me the job of naming you. Before we do that, I need one person to be the "guesser."** Choose someone to be the first guesser. [Guesser's name], **in a moment, you'll turn away from the group, close your eyes, and cover your ears so you won't hear what animal I'm telling the rest of the kids to be. I'll tap you on the shoulder when we're ready.** Don't have the guesser move yet, but tell the rest of the group: **After I whisper to the rest of you what animal to be, I'll tap the guesser's shoulder and have** [guesser's name] **turn around. We'll all say out loud, "One, two, three, guess which animal we might be!"** Have everyone repeat the rhyme with you. **Then everyone in the group will start acting like the animal I told you to be.** [Guesser's name] **will try to guess what animal you are!**

Have the guesser turn around, close his or her eyes, and cover his or her ears. Whisper the same animal name in each child's ear. Then tap the guesser's shoulder, have all kids say the rhyme with you, and let the children act out the animal until the guesser identifies it. Let several kids have turns being the guesser.

☆ ☆ ☆ ☆ ☆

At the end of the game, discuss the following questions:

• **How did you like acting out the animals God created?**

• **What do you think it was like for Adam to name all the new animals God created?**

Leader Tip

After you play the game awhile, let the past guesser become the new Adam. Be ready to help the child choose another animal and lead the others in saying the rhyme.

• When you were a guesser, how did you feel trying to name what kind of animals we were?

Say: **God created so many wonderful animals, and Adam did a great job naming them.** Go around the room and say each child's name. **God created each one of you in wonderful ways, too.**

We're Creative!

Topic: Creation

Scripture: Genesis 1:27

Game Overview: Kids will learn basic shapes as they create geometric figures.

☆ ☆ ☆ ☆ ☆

Supplies: Bible, scissors, construction paper

Preparation: Cut circles, squares, rectangles, and triangles from various colors of construction paper. Make enough so each child has a variety of shapes.

ather children in a circle, and teach them this rhyme:

> God made the sky and God made the sea;
> God made you and God made me.
>
> God made the animals; God made the trees;
> God made you and God made me.

Ask kids to tell you all kinds of things they know that God created. Then open your Bible to Genesis 1:27, and read aloud the words.

Say: **Our creative God made so many wonderful things. But you know what's really cool? God made us to be like him. We're creative too!**

Give each child a handful of shapes. Have kids arrange their shapes to create pictures of God's creation. For example, they could make trees, dogs, flowers, or people. "Show and tell" the creations, and then have children "erase" their pictures by scattering the shapes. Have them make new creations.

☆ ☆ ☆ ☆ ☆

At the end of the game, have kids leave their final creations in place. Gather around the creations, and discuss the following questions:

- What kinds of things did God create?
- What kinds of things did you create?

Ask all the creative kids to say the rhyme again! Have them clap to the beat as they say the words.

Daniel, the Lions Are Coming

Topic: Daniel

Scripture: Daniel 6

Game Overview: Kids will pretend to be lions and quietly creep up on Daniel in the den.

☆ ☆ ☆ ☆ ☆

Supplies: Bible

Preparation: Clear a large playing area.

Open a Bible to Daniel 6, and tell the kids about how God protected Daniel in the lions' den. Then choose one child to be Daniel, and have Daniel stand on one side of the room. Ask the other children to be lions and stand on the other side of the room.

Say: **When I say, "Daniel in the lions' den," Daniel, turn your back so you can't see the lions. Lions, quietly creep up to Daniel and try to touch Daniel's shoulder before he hears you. Daniel, if you hear a noise, turn around and point to the lion who made the noise. Then that lion will go back to the starting place, and everyone will say, "God protects Daniel!"** Have everyone shout the phrase. Say: **Daniel, if a lion actually touches your shoulder, turn around, give the lion a hug, and say, "God protects me!"** Have Daniel repeat the phrase. **Ready? Daniel in the lions' den!**

Play several rounds, and have the hugged lions become the next Daniels.

☆ ☆ ☆ ☆ ☆

At the end of the game, discuss the following questions:
- **Why couldn't the lions hurt Daniel?**
- **How does God protect you today?**

Say: **God protected Daniel, and God protects us today, too!**

Around in a Circle

Topic: Daniel

Scripture: Daniel 7:27b

Game Overview: Kids will obey the leader and learn to obey God.

☆ ☆ ☆ ☆ ☆

Supplies: Bible

Preparation: None needed

Use this game before you teach kids about Daniel, who obeyed God his whole life. Ask the kids to "obey" you first by forming a circle. Then have kids obey you again by singing the words and doing the actions you tell them to do. Sing these words to the tune of "Row, Row, Row Your Boat."

> **Skip, skip, skip and clap.** *(Have kids skip and clap as they move to the right in a circle.)*
> **Keep the circle round.**
> **Rub your knees** *(have kids rub their knees),*
> **Wave your arms** *(have kids wave their arms in the air),*
> **And then you touch the ground.** *(Have kids touch the ground with both hands.)*

> **Slide, slide, slide and clap.** *(Have kids slide in the circle to the left.)*
> **Then we'll do some more.** *(Keep sliding to the left.)*
> **Pull your ears** *(have kids gently pull both ears),*
> **Tap your foot** *(have kids tap one foot),*
> **And then you touch the floor.** *(Have kids touch the floor with both hands.)*

☆ ☆ ☆ ☆ ☆

At the end of the game, discuss the following questions:

· **Who did you obey during this game?**

· **How did you know what to do?**

Tell the kids how Daniel obeyed God all his life. Read aloud Daniel 7: 27b, and then say: **Daniel tells us in the Bible that everyone will obey God! We can obey God by doing what he tells us in the Bible to do.**

Leader Tip

Let children come up with new actions for more verses. Encourage them to take turns being the leader and having others obey them!

Small and Mighty

Topic: David

Scripture: 1 Samuel 17

Game Overview: Kids will toss soft "stones" at a high target to get an idea of what David's battle with Goliath might have been like.

✩ ✩ ✩ ✩ ✩

Supplies: Bible, paper plate, newspapers, masking tape, trash bags

Preparation: Use tape to mount the paper plate on a wall. For younger kids, place the plate at eye level; for older preschoolers, mount it about nine feet high. Use masking tape to mark a line a few feet away from the wall for the kids to stand behind.

> ## Leader Tip
> As kids play the game, you may vary the line's position, either closer to the wall or farther away from the wall.

Open your Bible to 1 Samuel 17, and briefly summarize the story of David and Goliath. Then let kids have some target practice. Demonstrate how to wad newspaper into a "stone," stand behind the line, and throw the paper at the target. Say: **OK! Now it's your turn to make your stones and throw them at the target. Pretend you're David aiming for Goliath.**

When you run out of newspaper, call a timeout and have kids help you sweep all the stones back behind the line.

✩ ✩ ✩ ✩ ✩

At the end of the game, have kids sweep the stones into a pile and form a circle around it. Hold a trash bag. As kids answer the following questions, have them toss the newspaper stones into the bag:

> ## Leader Tip
> Have all kids line up and fire their stones at one paper plate "Goliath," or tape several plates to the wall and have several Goliaths for kids to aim at.

• **What was it like for you to throw paper stones at the paper Goliath?**

• **How did God help David beat the giant?**

• **How does God help us live each day?**

Say a prayer of thanks to God who helped David and us, too.

Praise Sticks

Topic: David

Scripture: 2 Samuel 6

Game Overview: Kids will make musical instruments and play a game praising God.

☆ ☆ ☆ ☆ ☆

Supplies: Bible, washable markers, newspaper, and 6x½-inch dowels (two for each child)

Preparation: Cover a table with newspaper, and set out the markers and dowels.

O pen your Bible to 2 Samuel 6, and say: **King David and his people were having a good time praising God, because they knew God was with them. We can celebrate, too, by making praise sticks.**

Give each of the children two sticks, and have kids use the markers to decorate their sticks with colorful designs and patterns.

When children finish decorating their sticks, have them play a game, pretending to march behind David and praise God with him.

Ask children to line up behind you. Tell them to "follow the leader," and tap their sticks the same way you do. Say that when you want them to listen, you'll hold the sticks up in the air. Take the lead, and tap out a simple rhythm with your sticks. To begin, tap the sticks each time you take a step and say each word, "God is with us." Have the children follow your beat and say the words. When they've caught on to the concept, change the rhythm to double beats or triple beats while you march.

Leader Tip

Older preschoolers will enjoy taking the lead and picking a rhythm for the other children to copy. You could also try tapping out the rhythm of the words "Jerusalem," "Israelites," "David," and "Mephibosheth" (muh-FIB-uh-sheth).

☆ ☆ ☆ ☆ ☆

At the end of the game, discuss the following questions:

• **How did you like praising God with your instruments?**

• **Why should we praise God each day?**

Go around the circle and have kids each say one thing they want to praise God for. Help them tap out the rhythm of the words they say.

Who Will Lead?

Topic: Esther

Scripture: Esther 2:1-18

Game Overview: Kids will follow a leader, then switch and follow new leaders.

☆ ☆ ☆ ☆ ☆

Supplies: Bible

Preparation: Ask two teenagers or adults to help; then ahead of time, show them how to play the game.

Ask children to form a single file line. Position one leader at the end of the line, and another in the middle of the line. Tell children to follow the leader who's holding up his or her hand.

Stand at the head of the line, and hold up your hand. You'll be the first leader, and the line will march behind you. Start walking slowly and keep holding up your hand. Gradually increase your pace. After a minute of marching, lead kids in forming a circle so you're close to the leader you had placed at the end of the line. When you ask, "Who will lead?" have the leader at the end of the line hold up his or her hand as you take down yours.

Then step out of the line. That adult will become the new leader, and the kids will follow. Rejoin the line anywhere you'd like. After a few laps around the area, the new leader will ask, "Who will lead?" and the adult in the middle of the line will hold up a hand to become the third leader. The second leader will lower his or her hand.

Help kids scramble into a line after the third leader. Great confusion and noise will commence, and that's part of the fun. Direct kids and send them after the new leader. Have kids move into a circle again and slow the pace to cool down.

☆ ☆ ☆ ☆ ☆

Then sit in a circle, and discuss the following questions:

- **How did you know who to follow in this game?**
- **What was it like to follow new leaders?**

Open your Bible to Esther 2:1-18. Say: **The Bible tells us about King Xerxes who chose a new queen to help him lead.**

Briefly tell kids how Queen Esther helped save her people. Ask:

- **Why was Esther a good leader?**

Have kids clap for their good leaders who were so fun to follow!

The King's Scepter

Topic: Esther

Scripture: Esther 5:1-8

Game Overview: Kids will carefully watch the king's scepter and develop quick reactions.

☆ ☆ ☆ ☆ ☆

Supplies: Bible, baton or stick, paper crown or hat

Preparation: Clear a playing area.

Ask children to stand side by side along one wall. Have kids think of something they really want to tell you, such as something that happened to them last week. Tell them to not say their thoughts out loud yet. Hold the baton and the crown or hat, walk to the other wall, and face the kids.

Say: **When Queen Esther wanted to talk with the king, she had to wait until he held out his scepter to her, then she could walk over to him. A scepter is like a beautiful, gold stick. Let's pretend I'm King Xerxes.** Place the crown or hat on your head. **You can't come to talk to me until I hold out my scepter.** Hold up the baton. **You can walk forward, not run, only when I hold out my scepter. When I put it down, you must freeze.**

Start the game by holding up the scepter, and then put it down quickly. See how many kids are watching closely! If kids keep moving when the scepter is down, have them take three steps back. As kids get closer, hold the scepter high and let all of them come to you. Have everyone give a group hug. Play several times and let others take turns pretending to be the king.

☆ ☆ ☆ ☆ ☆

At the end of the game, have everyone gather in a circle. Open your Bible to Esther 5:1-8, and tell kids about Esther waiting to talk to the king about her plan to help her people. Discuss the following questions:

• **What did Queen Esther want to tell the king?**

• **What did you want to tell me at the beginning of the game?**

Pass the scepter, and let kids each share what they wanted to say.

Good Soil

Topic: Faith

Scripture: Luke 8:1-15

Game Overview: Kids will take on various roles in the parable of the sower.

✫ ✫ ✫ ✫ ✫

Supplies: Bible, beach balls (one for every four kids)

Preparation: Inflate the beach balls.

Tell kids the parable of the sower (Luke 8:1-15), and then have them play this game to act out the parable. Have kids form groups of four, and have each group make a small circle. Say: **I'm going to give you a motion to do. You'll use the motion to try to bat a beach ball around your group.**

Give each group a beach ball, and have all the members pretend to be birds. Have kids put their hands at their ribs and flap their arms like bird wings. They can use only their "wings" to bat the ball.

Play the game a second time and have kids pretend to be rocks. Rocks will put their hands at their sides and stand very still. They may use only their heads or shoulders to bat the ball.

Play the game a third time and have kids pretend to be thorns. Thorns will put their hands at their sides. They may use only their legs and feet to kick the ball.

Play the game a fourth time and have kids pretend to be good dirt. Good dirt will stand relaxed. Kids may use either their hands or their feet to bat the ball.

✫ ✫ ✫ ✫ ✫

At the end of the game, gather the balls and then discuss the following questions:

• **What role did you like best? Why?**

• **What was the easiest way to bat the ball?**

Say: **Good soil is best! When we're like good soil, we have faith in God and believe all he tells us in the Bible. We trust God and do what God wants each day of our lives.**

Shifting Sands

Topic: Faith

Scripture: Luke 6:46-49

Game Overview: Kids will use blocks as they learn about the wise and foolish builders.

★ ★ ★ ★ ★

Supplies: Bible, blocks, blanket, sheet of sturdy cardboard

Preparation: Lay the blanket and the cardboard on the ground, and set a bunch of blocks on each.

Say: **Let's work in two groups to build two houses out of blocks.** Motion for half of the kids to build a house on the blanket and the other half to build a house on the cardboard.

After the groups have built their houses, have them work together to carefully slide the blanket or cardboard and move their house across the room. See what happens!

★ ★ ★ ★ ★

At the end of the game, discuss the following questions:

  • **What happened when each group moved its house?**

  • **Which base was weaker? stronger?**

Tell kids the story of the wise and foolish builders (Luke 6:46-49).

Leader Tip

Even if both houses tumble during the move, it's OK. Make the connection that the cardboard is stronger than the blanket, but Jesus is the strongest foundation of all! Believe in Jesus!

Battered Boat

Topic: Faith

Scripture: Acts 27:13-26

Game Overview: Kids will join hands, pretending to be the boat in the stormy sea.

✯ ✯ ✯ ✯ ✯

Supplies: Bible, stopwatch

Preparation: Play in a gym or other large room free from obstacles.

Ask kids to form a circle in the middle of the room. Briefly tell them about Paul being on a boat in a terrible storm (Acts 27:13-26). Then have kids pretend they're on the boat with Paul.

Have kids join hands and walk toward a wall, still holding hands in a circle, until their "boat" circle touches a wall. Now the storm will begin, and the boat will begin to roll. Starting with the first child whose back touches the wall, rotate the entire circle so that each child's back touches the wall individually as kids move across the wall. When they get to the corner of the room, help the boat again move throughout the sea (open space) until it touches another wall. The storm will continue as the boat begins to roll again.

After kids practice rolling on the stormy seas, have kids hold hands in a circle in the center of the room. Time how long it takes them to walk to a wall, rotate the entire circle so that each child's back touches the wall individually, then move back to the center of the room. Play the game again, and have kids try to beat their time.

✯ ✯ ✯ ✯ ✯

At the end of the game, have kids sit in a circle and discuss the following questions:

• **What was it like for you to be tossed around in the stormy sea?**

• **Why was Paul not afraid during the storm in the story?**

Say: **Paul had faith that God would keep them safe. Just like Paul, we can have faith even when we go through bad times. God is always with us!**

Try the game again, and have kids sing while the circle moves through the center of the room. Sing to the tune of "Row, Row, Row Your Boat":

Row, row, row your boat
In the stormy sea.
I will not be afraid;
Jesus is with me!

Mirror Me!

Topic: Family

Scripture: 2 Timothy 1:5

Game Overview: Kids will learn a rhyme and "mirror" each other's actions.

☆ ☆ ☆ ☆ ☆

Supplies: Bible

Preparation: None needed

Have children sit so they face you. Have them imitate your actions as you recite this rhyme:

I look in the mirror, and what do I see? *(Cup hands next to eyes.)*
I see a happy face smiling at me. *(Smile broadly.)*
I look in the mirror, and what do I see? *(Cup hands next to eyes.)*
I see fingers waving at me. *(Wave fingers.)*
I look in the mirror, and what do I see? *(Cup hands next to eyes.)*
I see hands clapping for me. *(Clap hands.)*

Say: **I was an example, and you followed my actions. Now you can take turns doing the same thing with each other.**

Have kids form pairs and choose who will be the "example" and who will be the "follower." Have partners stand toe to toe, facing each other. Have followers mirror everything their partners do. Tell children to move slowly as they do actions such as patting their heads, touching their noses, or waving their hands.

After kids play for two minutes, have them switch roles.

☆ ☆ ☆ ☆ ☆

At the end of the game, discuss these questions:

• **Was it easier to be the example or the follower in our game? Why?**
• **What does it mean to be a good example to others?**

Read 2 Timothy 1:5, and tell kids Timothy's mother and grandmother were good examples to him for his faith. Ask kids to tell you about family members or church family members who are good examples to them. Encourage kids to be good examples, too.

Family Fame Game

Topic: Family

Scripture: Ephesians 3:14-15

Game Overview: Kids will share stories about family members.

☆ ☆ ☆ ☆ ☆

Supplies: Bible, dice, paper, pen

Preparation: For easy reference, write on a sheet of paper: "1 = mom or dad or guardian; 2 = grandparent or guardian; 3 = brother or sister or cousin; 4 = pet you have or wish you had; 5 = you; 6 = any memory of a family vacation or fun time."

Show kids the numbers on the dice, and then roll one to see what number comes up. Say: **Let's play a game in which we'll share stories about our families. When you roll the die, I'll tell you what to talk about.** Tell a quick family story that corresponds to the number you've rolled. For example, if you roll a number 2, tell about your grandma and why she was special to you.

Then have children take turns rolling a die. As each child rolls the die, encourage that child to tell a quick story. If kids need help, you could ask questions such as these: "Do you have a grandma or an older person who's special to you? What do you like about your grandma?" or "Have you seen any fun animals in the zoo that you wish you had as a pet? Tell us about the animal!"

☆ ☆ ☆ ☆ ☆

Leader Tip

Be aware of your children's family backgrounds. Not all come from a mom-dad-sibling type of family. Encourage kids to tell stories about people in their own families, different families, or in stories they've heard.

After everyone has had a turn, discuss the following questions:

- **Why are families important?**
- **How is our church like a family?**

Read aloud Ephesians 3:14-15, and then pray to thank God for all families— no matter what sizes or shapes they come in. Thank God especially for the church family.

Herding the Sheep

Topic: Following Jesus

Scripture: John 10:3b-4

Game Overview: Kids will make sheep, then play a "herding" game.

✩ ✩ ✩ ✩ ✩

Supplies: Empty toilet paper tubes, hole punch, cotton balls, glue, cotton swabs, scissors, yarn, black construction paper, newspaper

Preparation: Punch a hole in the end of each toilet paper tube, and tie one end of a six-foot length of yarn through the hole. Cut two ears for each sheep from the black construction paper (see illustration). Cover the art area with newspaper.

Set out the prepared toilet paper tubes. Show children how to use the cotton swabs to paint a thin layer of glue on the outside of the tubes. Then help children cover their tubes with one layer of cotton balls and attach the ears with glue. The ears should go on the same end of the tubes as the string. While kids work, have them think of names for their sheep. When they've covered the sheep with cotton and attached the ears, set the sheep aside to dry.

Read John 10:3b-4 to the kids. Say: **Good shepherds take care of their sheep. They know the names of their sheep, and their sheep follow them.** Go around the room and say each child's name. **Jesus is our good shepherd, and he knows each of us by name.** Have kids show one another the sheep they've made, then tell one another the names of their sheep.

When the sheep have dried, have kids play a "herding" game of tag. Ask children to walk around 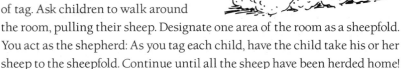 the room, pulling their sheep. Designate one area of the room as a sheepfold. You act as the shepherd: As you tag each child, have the child take his or her sheep to the sheepfold. Continue until all the sheep have been herded home!

✩ ✩ ✩ ✩ ✩

At the end of the game, discuss the following questions:

• **How can you take care of the sheep you've made?**

• **How is that like being a good shepherd to your sheep?**

• **How does Jesus, the very best shepherd, take care of you every day?**

Let kids hug their sheep and say a silent prayer of thanks for Jesus' love and care.

Come Along

Topic: Following Jesus

Scripture: Mark 1:14-20

Game Overview: Kids will play a choosing game and learn how Jesus chose the disciples who followed him.

☆ ☆ ☆ ☆ ☆

Supplies: Bible

Preparation: None needed

Tell kids the story of Jesus choosing his disciples and telling them to "Follow me" (Mark 1:14-20). Tell kids they'll play a game and be "chosen," too.

Help children form a circle and stand facing one direction. Ask each child to put his or her outside hand out.

Walk around the circle, and choose someone by taking his or her hand and saying, [Child's name], **follow me.** That child will hold your hand and walk with you, then catch another child's hand, and so on. Do this until everyone has been named and chosen, and then have everyone give the person in front of him or her a backrub.

Play again and have the last child chosen be the chooser. At the end of each "choosing," change the actions kids do to one another. Have them scratch a back, hug someone, give a handshake or a high five.

☆ ☆ ☆ ☆ ☆

At the end of the game, discuss the following questions:

· **What did you feel like when you were chosen and called by name?**

· **How can we follow Jesus every day?**

Say: **We can follow Jesus by learning about him and inviting friends to learn about him, too!**

Stop, Drop, and follow

Topic: Following Jesus

Scripture: Acts 9:1-20

Game Overview: Kids will discover what it was like for Saul to "see the light" and follow Jesus.

☆ ☆ ☆ ☆ ☆

Supplies: Bible, flashlight

Preparation: None needed

Tell kids about Saul seeing a light from heaven and deciding to follow Jesus (Acts 9:1-20). Have kids line up against a wall and pretend to be Saul.

Instruct them to drop to the ground when they see the flashlight shine, then stand up when they hear you say, **Saul! Saul! Why have you been mean to me?** Then have kids close their eyes, because Saul couldn't see either.

Tell children to follow your instructions with their eyes closed. Have them do a simple action, such as clapping their hands above their heads and saying, "Yea, Jesus," until you tell them to stop.

Ask children to open their eyes, see the flashlight shine on them, and play again as before. Each time, give different simple directions for kids to follow, such as stomping their feet in place and saying, "I love Jesus," or patting their heads with one hand and saying, "Jesus loves me."

☆ ☆ ☆ ☆ ☆

After the game, discuss the following questions:

• **What was it like to try to follow directions when you couldn't see?**

• **How do you think Saul felt when he suddenly couldn't see?**

• **What did Jesus want Saul to do?**

Say: **Always remember that Jesus wants you to follow him! To help others follow him, too, bring friends to church, and tell the people you meet how much Jesus loves them!**

friend! friend!

Topic: Friendship

Scripture: Proverbs 17:17a

Game Overview: Kids will listen to friends' hearts in this active game.

☆ ☆ ☆ ☆ ☆

Supplies: Bible, cardboard tubes

Preparation: None needed

G ive each child an empty cardboard tube. Have kids form pairs and listen to their partners' hearts through the tubes. Then call out an action such as "jump." After kids have jumped for a few seconds, call out, "Friend! Friend!" Have kids stop moving and listen to their partners' hearts through the tubes.

Ask partners to give each other a hug and tell each other, "I'm glad God made you my friend!" Then have kids find new partners and do another active motion, such as "run in place." After a few seconds, call out, "Friend! Friend!" and have kids listen to their new partners' hearts. Ask partners to give each other a hug and tell each other, "I'm glad God made you my friend!" Continue this until kids have heard the hearts of and affirmed several friends.

☆ ☆ ☆ ☆ ☆

At the end of the game, read aloud Proverbs 17:17a and then discuss the following questions:

• **What did you like about this game?**

• **How did you like getting and giving hugs to your friends?**

• **What do you like most about your friends?**

Say: **God has blessed us so much by giving us good friends. We can show our love to our friends by giving them hugs and saying nice things to them. I'm glad God made each one of you!**

Feather Toss

Topic: Friendship

Scripture: 1 Thessalonians 5:11

Game Overview: Kids will show encouraging actions to their friends before a feather touches the ground.

☆ ☆ ☆ ☆ ☆

Supplies: Bible, craft feather or facial tissue

Preparation: None needed

Ask children to scatter throughout the room. Call out one of the actions below, and toss a feather or facial tissue into the air. Have all the children do the action while the feather floats in the air. When the feather touches the ground, have children freeze in place. Then toss the feather again, and call out another action. Try these actions and sounds:

- **Pat someone's back and say, "Jesus loves you!"**
- **Rub someone's shoulders and say, "It'll be OK."**
- **Hold someone's hand and jump up and down.**
- **Clap your hands against someone else's hands and laugh out loud.**
- **Shake someone's hand and smile.**

Let kids take turns tossing the feather or tissue. Help them think of "friendly" actions and words to call out.

☆ ☆ ☆ ☆ ☆

At the end of the game, discuss the following questions:

- **What fun things did you just do with your friends?**
- **What other fun things do friends do together?**

Read 1 Thessalonians 5:11, and then toss the feather or tissue one more time. Say: **Hug someone and say, "Thanks for being my friend!"**

Who's That?

Topic: Friendship

Scripture: John 15:15b

Game Overview: Kids will stand back to back and try to guess who's behind them.

☆ ☆ ☆ ☆ ☆

Supplies: Bible

Preparation: None needed

Have kids form two groups. Have the first group stand facing a wall and the other group quietly stand back to back with the first group. The children facing the wall shouldn't know who's behind them.

Have the first group of children reach over their shoulders and each try to recognize who's behind them by touching the person's head. Give children in the first group two guesses before they turn around to see who's behind them. Then have partners tell each other their names and one thing they like to do with a friend.

Then have kids switch places. Have the second group of children face the wall while the first group mixes itself up and quietly stands back to back with the second group.

☆ ☆ ☆ ☆ ☆

At the end of the game, discuss the following questions:

• **How many of you knew your friends just by touching their heads?**

• **What did you find out from talking with your friends just now?**

Read John 15:15b. Then ask:

• **Who else is our friend?**

Close by having everyone shout, "Jesus is our friend!"

Who Do You Love?

Topic: God's love

Scripture: Psalm 117:1-2

Game Overview: Kids will express love for one another in this fast-paced game and hear how God loves us all.

☆ ☆ ☆ ☆ ☆

Supplies: Bible

Preparation: None needed

Have children sit in a circle. Read Psalm 117:1-2, and say: **Let's play a game to tell about our love for one another and about God's love for all of us!** Choose a child to sit in the middle. Have that child point to another child and ask, "Who do you love?" The child will answer by pointing to another child in the circle and saying, "I love [child's name]." Then the

> ## Leader Tip
> Vary the action in the game by having kids crawl, scoot on their bottoms, or hop on both feet.

two children sitting in the circle will jump up and switch places. The child in the middle of the circle will try to get to one of the open places in the circle before the other two children do. If the child in the middle asks, "Who loves us all?" have the children respond, "God does!" Then have everyone jump up, run around the circle once, give a group hug, and then sit down. Have children play until everyone has had a chance to be in the middle of the circle.

☆ ☆ ☆ ☆ ☆

At the end of the game, discuss the following questions:

• **How did it feel to get a hug after every time you shouted, "God does"?**

• **Who tells you about God's love?**

• **Who can you tell about God's love?**

Say: **God's love feels so good. Let's tell others about God's love for them, too!**

Lost Sheep

Topic: God's love

Scripture: Luke 15:1-7

Game Overview: Kids will search for lost "sheep" and learn how each person is precious to God.

☆ ☆ ☆ ☆ ☆

Supplies: Bible

Preparation: Turn a table on its side.

Read Luke 15:1-7 to the children, and tell them about the parable of the lost sheep. Say: **God loves each one of us so much. God is like a shepherd who has lost one sheep. He'll go after the sheep and look and look until he finds it. Then the shepherd will be so happy for that one little sheep that was lost but now is found.**

Ask everyone to bleat like sheep so kids can hear their best sheep voices! Then have kids all close their eyes. Tap one person on the shoulder, and have that person hide behind an overturned table. Ask the others to open their eyes and guess which sheep is missing.

Start again by having everyone bleat like sheep. Then have kids close their eyes so you can choose the next sheep to be lost and then found. Play several times so lots of kids have the chance to be lost and then found.

☆ ☆ ☆ ☆ ☆

At the end of the game, discuss the following questions:

• **How did you feel when you were by yourself behind the table?**

• **How did you feel when you were found by the others?**

Say: **When we sin or do bad things, we can feel lost and alone. God loves us so much that he gave us Jesus. Because of Jesus, we'll live forever in heaven. That makes all of us happy!**

God's Loving Plans

Topic: God's love

Scripture: Jeremiah 29:11-13

Game Overview: Kids will follow the leader's plans and find missing envelopes.

☆ ☆ ☆ ☆ ☆

Supplies: Bible, envelopes, masking tape, scissors, red construction paper

Preparation: Draw a large heart on a sheet of red construction paper. Cut the heart picture into ten large pieces, and place each piece in a separate envelope. Tape half of the envelopes in obvious places, such as on the wall, on top of tables, or on windows. Tape the rest of the envelopes in less obvious places, such as inside cabinet doors or under chair seats.

Gather children and say: **Special envelopes are hidden around the room. Each envelope has part of a message inside. We're going to hunt for all the envelopes to find out what the message is. First, let's make a plan to help us find all the envelopes.** Ask:

• **What are some ways we can get to the envelopes?** Children might mention things such as walking, running, hopping, crawling, or tiptoeing.

Say: **Some of the envelopes will be easy to find—you can probably see them right now! But other envelopes will be harder to find. You'll need to follow my plan to find them all so we can hear the special message.**

Lead children around the room, traveling in the different ways that children have mentioned. You might also have children count their steps, walk around furniture, crawl under a table, move like animals, or walk sideways. Allow a different child to retrieve each envelope and hand it to you.

☆ ☆ ☆ ☆ ☆

After all the envelopes have been found, let children work together to tape the pieces to form the heart. When kids have finished the picture, ask:

• **What is God's message to us?**

• **How does God show his love to you?**

• **How do you show your love to God?**

Read Jeremiah 29:11-13 to the kids, and then say: **The Bible tells us God loves us and has good plans for us. If you hadn't followed my plans, you wouldn't have found all the envelopes. If we don't follow God's good plans, we'll miss out on all the great things he may have for us.**

Powerful Protection

Topic: God's power

Scripture: Jeremiah 16:19a

Game Overview: Kids will build a strong fortress and talk about God's power.

☆ ☆ ☆ ☆ ☆

Supplies: Bible, blocks, boxes, blankets, cardboard, stopwatch

Preparation: Place all the supplies in the center of the room.

Gather kids around the supplies, and ask:

• **Where do you go when you're afraid? Why?**

Say: **The Bible talks about a strong place called a fortress,** where people would go when they were afraid. A fortress was a strong tower—kind of like a castle. Let's see what the Bible says about a fortress. Read Jeremiah 16:19a from an easy-to-understand Bible translation. Ask:

• **How is God like a strong fortress?**

Say: **This verse tells us that God is like a strong, safe place we can go to when we're afraid. God wants us to feel secure and protected, as if we were in a mighty castle. To remember that God is our fortress, let's use these supplies and build a fortress right here in our room! We have two minutes to build. Ready? Go!**

☆ ☆ ☆ ☆ ☆

> ### Leader Tip
> You may want to bring in pictures of castles and real fortresses. Point out to children that, as strong as those buildings appear, they're no match for the power of God!

Give kids two minutes to build a "fortress." Help children drape the blankets over tables and chairs. Call time, and then let kids climb inside. Ask:

• Is this a mighty fortress? Why or why not?

• What can we do to make it stronger?

Give children two more minutes to stack blocks, boxes, or sheets of card-board against the sides of the fortress to make it stronger. Gather everyone inside and ask:

• Now is this a mighty fortress? Why or why not?

• Who would be able to tear down our fortress?

Say: We can't make a fortress that's as strong as God. God is power-ful and will use his power to protect us!

Give kids two minutes to tear down the fortress, and several more minutes to clean up!

Power Racing

Topic: God's power

Scripture: Psalm 68:34-35

Game Overview: Kids will race once holding toilet paper, another time holding a stick, and then compare the two.

☆ ☆ ☆ ☆ ☆

Supplies: Bible, toilet paper, yardsticks or dowels

Preparation: Tear toilet paper into eight-inch lengths. You'll need one length of toilet paper and one yardstick or dowel for each pair.

Have kids form pairs, and give each pair a strand of toilet paper. Have partners each hold an end of the strip of toilet paper. Ask all the pairs to stand along one side of the room. When you say "Go," have pairs race across the room and back, holding the paper between them without breaking it. If partners break their strand, the pair must go back to the beginning and restart the course with a fresh strand of toilet paper.

Clap for all the runners, and then have kids play again. This time, give each pair a sturdy stick such as a dowel or yardstick. Have partners each hold one end of the stick. On "Go," have them run across the room and back.

☆ ☆ ☆ ☆ ☆

At the end of the games, discuss the following questions:

• **What happened as you ran both races?**

• **Which was stronger, the toilet paper or the stick?**

Read Psalm 68:34-35, and say: **God is like the yardstick. God is more powerful and stronger than anything on earth. Let's tell everyone wherever we go about God's awesome power!**

Jesus Loves You

Topic: Jesus' birth

Scripture: Luke 2:1-20

Game Overview: Kids will hear the story about Jesus' birth, then sing a song and play a game to celebrate.

☆ ☆ ☆ ☆ ☆

Supplies: Bible

Preparation: None needed

Read about Jesus' birth from an easy-to-understand children's Bible (Luke 2:1-20). Then ask these questions:

• **What's your favorite part about the story of Jesus' birth? Why?**

• **Why did God send his Son, Jesus, to be born on earth?**

Say: **I love the story of Jesus' birth! God loves us so much that he sent Jesus to be born on earth. Because of Jesus, we'll live forever!**

Gather kids in a circle, and choose a child to stand in the middle. Have children hold hands as you sing this song with them to the tune of "Clementine":

Jesus loves you. Jesus loves you.
Jesus loves you as you are.
Thank you, God, for baby Jesus
And his love forevermore.

As you sing the first two lines, have the group walk to the center of the circle until they've formed a tight group around the child in the middle to hug him or her. As you sing the last two lines, have children back up. Then sing the song again and have the hugged child walk around the outside of the circle, tapping kids' shoulders to the beat. The last child he or she touches will go into the middle of the circle and will be the next child to get hugged as kids sing the song again. Continue playing the game until lots of kids have been hugged and get to choose the next ones to be in the middle.

Guiding Star

Topic: Jesus' birth
Scripture: Matthew 2:1-12
Game Overview: Kids will follow a light until they find the baby Jesus.

☆ ☆ ☆ ☆ ☆

Supplies: Bible, flashlight, baby doll
Preparation: Hide the baby doll somewhere in the room.

Tell kids about the bright star that led some followers to find the baby Jesus (Matthew 2:1-12). Then play a game in which kids follow a light and find baby Jesus, too.

Turn on the flashlight, and turn off the lights. Shine the flashlight all around the room as you lead kids in following its light. Eventually shine the light where you've hidden the baby doll.

Turn on the lights, and have kids close their eyes. Help a child hide the baby Jesus, and then have the other kids open their eyes. Have the child who hid the doll shine the flashlight to lead the others to the hiding spot.

Play the game several times, letting several children hide the baby and lead the others with the flashlight beam.

☆ ☆ ☆ ☆ ☆

At the end of the game, discuss the following questions:
• **How did you feel when you were following the light?**
• **How did you feel when you found the baby?**
Say: **It must have been so exciting to follow the real star to Bethlehem to find baby Jesus. I'm so glad Jesus was born!**

Bearing Gifts

Topic: Jesus' birth

Scripture: Matthew 2:1-12

Game Overview: Kids will be camels and wise men as they bring gifts to Jesus.

✭ ✭ ✭ ✭ ✭

Supplies: Bible, lunch sacks, jelly beans, tape or stapler

Preparation: Fill lunch sacks with small handfuls of jelly beans. Fold the top of the bags down, and tape or staple them shut. You'll need a "treasure bag" for each child. Lay the treasure bags along one side of the room.

Have kids form trios and line up along the wall where you've placed the treasure bags. Open your Bible to Matthew 2:1-12, and say: **The Bible tells us that after Jesus was born, Magi, or wise men, traveled a long way to bring him wonderful gifts. In this game, let's pretend to be wise men, bringing gifts on our camels! But first, you'll need to choose someone in your group to be the camel.**

Instruct the camels to get on their hands and knees. Have two wise men stand on either side of each camel and place one treasure bag on the camel's back. When you say, "Onward to Bethlehem!" have the camels crawl and the wise men walk as they carefully deliver their treasure bag to the opposite side of the room. Have the wise men help keep the bags from falling off of the camels' back. The wise men will set the bags on the floor, and then the trios will travel back to get another treasure bag. Let a different child in each trio be the camel on each trip. Continue the game until each trio has delivered three treasure bags.

✭ ✭ ✭ ✭ ✭

At the end of the game, discuss these questions:

• **What gifts did the Magi give to the baby Jesus?**

• **If you had been there when Jesus was born, what gift would you have given him?**

Have each of the children open a treasure bag and enjoy its contents. As kids eat each jelly bean, have them say a gift they'd give baby Jesus. Close with a prayer, thanking God for sending us the best gift of all—Jesus!

Feed a Face

Topic: Jesus' miracles

Scripture: Luke 9:12-17

Game Overview: Kids will see how many snacks they can "feed" into a huge mouth.

☆ ☆ ☆ ☆ ☆

Supplies: Bible, appliance box, scissors, marker, packets of snacks

Preparation: Use a marker to draw a large face on a large appliance box. Cut out a huge mouth. Set packets of snacks several feet away from the box. You'll need at least one packet of snacks per child.

Gather kids in front of the box. Have them take turns tossing the packets of snacks into the mouth to see how many packets they can get through the mouth. Then gather the packets, and have kids try again. See whether they can increase the number of packets that make it through the mouth.

☆ ☆ ☆ ☆ ☆

At the end of the game, discuss the following questions:

• **How many packets did you all "feed" through the mouth in the game?**

• **Was it easy or hard for you to do? Explain.**

Tell kids about a time when Jesus fed 5,000 mouths (Luke 9:12-17)! Have kids celebrate Jesus' miracle by opening the packets and eating the snacks!

Heal Our Friend!

Topic: Jesus' miracles

Scripture: Matthew 9:1-8

Game Overview: Each child will work with a partner and carry a friend to Jesus to be healed.

☆ ☆ ☆ ☆ ☆

Supplies: Bible, towels, dolls

Preparation: Lay the towels along one wall of the room. Put a doll on top of each towel. You'll need one towel and a doll for every two kids.

Help children gather in pairs along one wall of the play area. Read Matthew 9:1-8, which tells about a person who couldn't walk. His friends brought him to Jesus to be healed.

Instruct partners to each hold an end of the towel so they can carry the doll. Go to the opposite wall, and then say: **When I say, "Come to me," carry your doll to me. When you get here, I'll say, "Get up and walk." Leave your towel, and then each of you hold one of your doll's hands and walk it back to the starting line. Ready? Come to me!**

Play the game several times, letting other children act as Jesus to say "Come to me" and "Get up and walk."

☆ ☆ ☆ ☆ ☆

At the end of the game, discuss the following questions:

• **In this game, how did you feel as you brought your friend to be healed?**

• **How do you think the friends felt when Jesus healed the person who couldn't walk?**

Say: **Jesus is God's Son. He did many miracles like making the lame man walk. Many people praised God because Jesus did such great things.**

Leader Tip

Instead of dolls, you could also inflate and tie off balloons. Draw a face on each balloon, and have pairs carry the balloon friends during the game.

Gimme a Hand

Topic: Jesus' miracles

Scripture: Mark 3:1-5

Game Overview: Each child will draw with a sock on his or her hand, then take it off and draw again.

✩ ✩ ✩ ✩ ✩

Supplies: Bible, two socks, chalk, chalkboard (or markers and two large sheets of paper)

Preparation: Set up the supplies along one wall of the playing area.

Have children form two teams and stand in two lines facing the chalkboard. Have the first person in line put a sock over his or her hand.

Tell kids the story of the man with the shriveled hand (Mark 3:1-5). Say: **Let's race to make a drawing of what this man must have felt like with a hand that wouldn't work! I'll tell you what to draw. The first people in line will draw first, then go back to your team, give the next person in line the sock to put on, and so on. We'll keep going until everyone has had a turn to wear the sock and try to draw.**

Call out the following things for the kids to draw: "Make a circle to be the man's head," "Draw a frown on his face," "Draw two eyes," "Draw a nose," "Draw two ears," and "Draw some hair."

✩ ✩ ✩ ✩ ✩

When everyone has had a turn, ask:

• **What was it like for you to draw with a sock on your hand?**

Say: **It was hard for the man to do anything with his shriveled hand. That must have made him sad. But Jesus told him to stretch out his hand, and it was healed.** Have kids stretch out their hands in front of them and wiggle their fingers. **That must have made the man happy. Jesus did many miracles because he is God's Son.**

Play again without the socks. Tell kids what to draw, but instead of the frowns have them draw smiles.

The Bear in Heaven

Topic: Jesus' resurrection

Scripture: John 3:16

Game Overview: Kids will bounce a bear on a blanket and learn about heaven and Jesus' resurrection.

✩ ✩ ✩ ✩ ✩

Supplies: Bible, blanket, teddy bear

Preparation: None needed

Leader Tip

If you have fifteen or more kids, consider dividing the group into teams to see which team can achieve the most unusual teddy bear toss. Of course, you should give the teddy bear a nickname!

Spread the blanket on the ground, and have kids stand around it. Have them slightly roll up the blanket's edges and get a good grip on it. Place the teddy bear in the center of the blanket, and announce that kids will try to toss the bear high enough to go to heaven.

After having the whole group yell, "One, two, three—go to heaven!" have everyone pull back on the blanket at the same time to toss the teddy bear in the air. Encourage kids to repeat this several times, trying to achieve higher and higher tosses.

✩ ✩ ✩ ✩ ✩

At the end of the game, have kids lay the blanket on the floor and sit around it. Then discuss the following questions:

• **What do you think heaven is like?**

• **How do we get to heaven?**

Read aloud John 3:16; then say: **Even though we tried and tried, we couldn't get the bear to go to heaven! We get to heaven one way—through Jesus. Because we believe Jesus took our sins with him to the cross, then rose from the dead, we'll live with him forever in heaven!**

Leader Tip

Several Bible references have given people the idea that heaven is "up." For example, Matthew 28:2 ("for an angel of the Lord came *down* from heaven"); Matthew 28:6 ("He is not here; he has *risen*"); and Mark 16:19 ("After the Lord Jesus had spoken to them, he was *taken up* into heaven").

Resurrection Relay

Topic: Jesus' resurrection

Scripture: John 20:1-18

Game Overview: Kids will play a running relay to mimic the way everyone ran to share the good news of Jesus' power.

☆ ☆ ☆ ☆ ☆

Supplies: Bible, inner tube

Preparation: Clear a playing area, and place the inner tube on one side of the room. You could use a hula hoop or large ball instead of an inner tube.

Tell kids about Jesus' death and resurrection. Focus on how the disciples heard about the stone being rolled away and ran to check it out (John 20:1-18).

Then ask kids to form two lines on opposite sides of the room. Tell children to pretend that the inner tube is the stone that was rolled away from the tomb. Instruct the first child in one line to roll the stone to the other line and hand it to the first person in that line. The first "roller" will go to the end of that line, as the new roller goes to the other side, repeating the process. As kids roll the inner tube to the other side, have them shout, "Jesus is alive!"

☆ ☆ ☆ ☆ ☆

At the end of the game, discuss the following questions:

• **How do you think the disciples felt when they found out Jesus was alive?**

• **Who can you tell today that Jesus is alive?**

Say: **Jesus died and rose again. Jesus is alive! Because of Jesus, we'll live forever. What good news!**

Joseph's Beautiful Coat

Topic: Joseph

Scripture: Genesis 37

Game Overview: Kids will make their own "coat of many colors."

☆ ☆ ☆ ☆ ☆

Supplies: Bible, grocery sacks, scissors, washable markers, CD player, Christian music CD

Preparation: Cut slits up the fronts of grocery bags. Cut neck holes in the top of the bags and armholes in the sides to make "coats." Make a coat for each child. Decorate one coat, and have it handy for the first part of the game.

Bring out the decorated coat, and say: **In Genesis 37, the Bible tells us about Joseph. His dad loved Joseph more than any of his brothers, so his dad gave only Joseph a beautiful coat.** Put on the coat, and turn in a circle as if you were modeling it. Ask:

• **If you were Joseph, how would you feel about getting such a great gift?**

• **If you were Joseph's brothers, how would you feel about** *not* **getting a gift at all?**

cut

Say: **Joseph's brothers were so jealous that they sold Joseph to some people who were leaving their country. The story does have a happy ending, because God is in control. Joseph ended up leading people and saving many lives. Instead of just me having a cool coat, I want each of you to have one, too!**

Have each child put on a paper coat, and give each child a washable marker. Play music and have children march around the room. Stop the music, and have each child find a partner and then draw simple designs on each other's coats. After a few seconds, start the music again. Continue until the children's coats are full of colorful designs. Have kids wear their coats and sing a song of praise to God, who made the story of Joseph have a happy ending!

Leader Tip

Instead of making coats out of bags and markers, you could use real coats or sweaters and have kids use clothespins to attach streamers to the coats.

Joseph's Journey

Topic: Joseph

Scripture: Genesis 37–45

Game Overview: Kids will walk in Joseph's footsteps down a winding road.

☆ ☆ ☆ ☆ ☆

Supplies: Bible, masking tape, rope, broom, chair, paper crown, stopwatch

Preparation: Set up a four-station course consisting of a four-foot strip of masking tape, followed by a circle made from a rope, then a broom, and finally a chair with a paper crown sitting on it. Make the stations far enough apart so that children have to take several steps between stations.

Ask kids to line up single file in front of the first station. Say: **Let's walk through Joseph's life together. I'll tell you the story as we walk through the course. Let's time ourselves to see how long it takes us to walk through the story and the course. Repeat the words and actions after me.** Start the stopwatch, and proceed with the story.

Joseph walked a long, long way *(walk on the masking tape)*,
Got thrown into a well. *(Jump into the rope circle, and crouch down.)*
His brothers didn't like him *(shake your head, and make taunting faces)*,
As anyone could tell! *(Hold out both hands and shrug shoulders.)*

He worked for Egypt's rulers *(sweep with the broom)*,
Got thrown into a jail. *(Crouch down behind the chair.)*
But he became a ruler *(put the crown on)*,
'Cause God can never fail! *(Throw up both arms.)*

After everyone has followed you through the course, stop the stopwatch and see how long it took. Have everyone shake hands with someone standing close by. Say: **The handshake shows that Joseph and his brothers finally got back together again, which made them all very happy.**

Time the game again, repeating the words and actions more quickly. See how fast kids can complete the course.

☆ ☆ ☆ ☆ ☆

At the end of the game, discuss the following questions:
• **What did you like about going on Joseph's journey?**
• **How do you think Joseph felt when he got thrown into a well?**

Go around to each station and ask kids how they think Joseph felt at that point in his journey. Then say: **God helped the brothers get back together and forgive one another. The next time you think a lot of bad things are happening to you, remember Joseph. God helped Joseph, and God helps you, too. God makes good things happen.**

Smiles of Joy

Topic: Joy

Scripture: Isaiah 49:13

Game Overview: Kids will pass a smile, shout for joy, and burst into song.

☆ ☆ ☆ ☆ ☆

Supplies: Bible

Preparation: None needed

Read Isaiah 49:13 to the kids; then say: **The person who wrote this verse wanted to shout for joy and burst into song each time he thought about God. Let's spread some joy since we have such a great God!**

Have kids form two groups and sit in two lines. Instruct the first person in each line to make a happy, silly face and show it to the person behind him or her. That person will imitate the face and show it to the person behind him or her until the face has gotten all the way to the end of the line. The person at the end of the line will run up to the beginning of the line and make a different face. Continue playing until everyone has had a turn.

Say: **What a lot of smiles you made! Now, let's play again. This time pass a happy face down your line as you "shout for joy" by saying, "God is great!"** Play again, and have kids pass smiles and shouts of joy.

☆ ☆ ☆ ☆ ☆

At the end of the game, discuss the following questions:

• **Why do you love God?**

• **What are some of the things God has blessed you with?**

Say: **God loves us and gives us good gifts like family, church, the beautiful creation, animals, and friends! When I think about God, I want to shout with joy and burst into song!**

Lead everyone in singing a joyful song such as "My God Is So Great."

Joy Cards

Topic: Joy

Scripture: Psalm 119:111

Game Overview: Kids will play a joyful guessing game with edible "cards."

☆ ☆ ☆ ☆ ☆

Supplies: Bible; spoons; instant vanilla pudding; quart-sized, resealable freezer bags; milk; measuring cups and spoons; plastic spoons; washrags

Preparation: Set out the supplies.

Give each child a resealable freezer bag. Into each bag, pour one-fourth cup of milk and two tablespoons of instant vanilla pudding mix. Release the excess air from the bags and seal them; then wipe them off with the washrag if anything has spilled on the outside. Have children knead their bags to mix the ingredients. The pudding will quickly get thick to create "joy cards."

When children have finished making their cards, have them sit in a circle on the floor, setting their cards in front of them. Direct children to spread the pudding inside the bag so it forms a flat, even layer. Ask:

• **How do you look when you're happy?**

After kids smile at you, have them use their fingers to draw a smile on their joy cards. Have kids "erase" the cards by gently spreading the pudding flat again. Then ask:

• **What makes you happy?**

After kids tell you things such as "My mom loves me," "My dog's tricks," "Food," and so on, have them use their fingers to draw what makes them happy on their cards. For example, they could draw a heart or a dog or a candy bar. One at a time, have kids show their cards while the others guess what they've drawn. The person who correctly guesses first gets to be the next one to show his or her card. After everyone has shown and guessed the cards, ask:

• **You know what makes me really happy?**

Hold up a Bible and say: **God's Word makes me happy. Listen to what the Bible says.** Read Psalm 119:111. **The person who wrote this verse was happy that God guided him forever. God's rules and word were the joy of his heart.**

Have kids draw a cross or a Bible "book" shape on their cards and then each say one thing about God that makes them happy or filled with joy. Give each child a spoon, and let children open their bags and eat the contents of their cards.

Yards of Smiles

Topic: Joy

Scripture: Job 8:21

Game Overview: Kids will measure their smiles and spread their joy.

☆ ☆ ☆ ☆ ☆

Supplies: Bible, several rolls of Fruit by the Foot or bubble gum that comes in the measuring tape packets

Preparation: Have one foot of treats for each person.

Have everyone sit in a circle facing one another. Say: **The Bible tells us to be joyful and to spread our joy wherever we go. Show everyone how you look when you're filled with joy.** Watch kids smile. **OK, now show everyone your biggest smiles!** Watch kids give you big, big smiles. **Wow! Great smiles! Let's all be "smile-o-meters" and measure those smiles.**

Use some Fruit by the Foot to measure a child's smile. Tear off that length, and give it to that child who will then measure the child's smile next to him or her. Continue until everyone has measured a neighbor's smile and is holding a length of Fruit by the Foot.

Place the "smiles" end to end on a table.

☆ ☆ ☆ ☆ ☆

At the end of the game, discuss the following questions:

· **What makes you happy or joyful?**

· **How big do you think God's smile is when he thinks of you?**

Have your class use one long piece of Fruit by the Foot for God's smile and place it by the other fruity smiles. Then bring out more of the treats and let everyone eat!

Breezy Kind Time

Topic: Kindness
Scripture: Colossians 3:12
Game Overview: Kids will enjoy being part of a breezy game.

✭ ✭ ✭ ✭ ✭

Supplies: Bible, marker, old bedsheet, CD player, Christian music CD
Preparation: Draw a happy face near the edge of an old bedsheet. Set up the CD.

Lay the bedsheet on the ground, and have children stand around it. Ask them to hold it waist-high with both hands. Play music and have children pass the sheet hand to hand around the circle. Stop the music, and have whoever is closest to the happy face sit underneath the sheet in the middle of the circle. Ask the other children to gently raise and lower the sheet so they treat the child underneath to a gentle breeze. While the children raise and lower the sheet, have them say, "Here's a soft and gentle breeze. Just for you, it's sure to please." Then go around the circle and have each child say one kind thing to the person in the middle. Have that child rejoin the circle. Play music and continue the game until everyone has had a chance to enjoy the gentle breeze and hear kind words.

✭ ✭ ✭ ✭ ✭

At the end of the game, discuss the following questions:

· **How did we show kindness in the game?**
· **How do you show kindness to others every day?**

Say: **We can show kindness through gentle actions like hugs and gentle words like "I love you." God wants us to be kind to everyone.**

Read Colossians 3:12 to the kids; then have them give a kind hug or handshake to five others in the room.

Leader Tip

If you don't have an old bedsheet, an old tablecloth or an inexpensive plastic tablecloth would work well, too.

A Kind Touch

Topic: Kindness

Scripture: 1 Thessalonians 5:15

Game Overview: Kids will play a "kind" variation of "Heads Up, Seven Up."

☆ ☆ ☆ ☆ ☆

Supplies: Four feathers

Preparation: None needed

Ask kids to sit in a circle. Show them how to lightly brush someone's forearm with a feather, and say: **Isn't that a nice, gentle, kind action?** Pass the feather around the circle, and let each child brush his or her neighbor's arm with it. As each child's arm gets brushed, have him or her say "Ah-h-h-h-h." **Let's use this kind action in a game.**

Choose four children, and ask them to stand in front of the room. Give each of them a feather. Have the other children lie face down on the floor with their eyes closed and their faces hidden in the crooks of their elbows. Ask the kids with the feathers to quietly walk through the room and each lightly brush one child's forearm. As soon as they've each brushed someone's arm, have them return to the front of the room. Then ask the other children to sit up. If a feather brushed them, have them stand up. One by one, call on them to identify who they think touched them. Don't tell them who touched them with a feather until each one has guessed. Then have the feather holders walk to the ones they've touched and give them hugs. Have those kids switch places, and then play again. Have the new feather holders choose new kids to gently touch with a feather. Play until everyone has had a turn. Each time kids reveal who they've touched with a feather, have them do another kind action, such as pat a back, smile and wave, or give a high five.

☆ ☆ ☆ ☆ ☆

At the end of the game, discuss the following questions:

· **What kind actions did you show in the game?**
· **What kind actions can you show at home?**

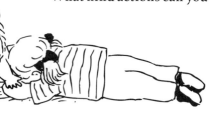

The Name Game

Topic: Loving others

Scripture: John 10:3

Game Overview: Kids will play a name game and learn that knowing people's names is one way to show love to them.

☆ ☆ ☆ ☆ ☆

Supplies: Bible

Preparation: None needed

Ask children to sit in a circle. Open a Bible to John 10:3, and read it out loud to the children. Say: **God loves us so much that he calls us by name. We can show love to others when we know their names. Let's play a game in which we call one another by name.**

Encourage children to join you in a steady clap. Call out children's names, and have the class mimic the way you call them out. Make sure you call each child's name at least once. Say names in these ways:

- whispering
- shouting
- singing
- speaking in a low voice
- speaking in a high voice
- saying a name slowly
- saying a name quickly
- saying two names right after each other

☆ ☆ ☆ ☆ ☆

At the end of the game, discuss these questions:

- **How does calling someone by name show that person you love him or her?**
- **What other ways can you show people you love them?**

Say: **We feel good when people call us by name, instead of just saying, "Hey, you over there!" We can also show people we love them by hugging, kissing, and being kind and helpful. God wants us to love others!**

Jesus Loves Us

Topic: Loving others

Scripture: 1 Corinthians 13:13

Game Overview: Kids will play a game, sending people from one group to another for signs of love.

☆ ☆ ☆ ☆ ☆

Supplies: Bible

Preparation: Clear a playing area.

Have children form two groups and line up on opposite sides of the room. Have one group pick a child from the opposite group. For example, the group might choose Stephen. Then have the children call out, "Jesus loves us; this we know. Send Stephen over, and we'll tell him so." Have Stephen run over to the group that called him. Then the children will surround him with a group hug and say, "Jesus loves you, Stephen."

Let the other group choose a child to come over for a hug. Continue the game until everyone has been shown Jesus' love.

☆ ☆ ☆ ☆ ☆

At the end of the game, discuss the following questions:

• **How did we show Jesus' love to others in this game?**

• **Why does Jesus want us to love others?**

Read 1 Corinthians 13:13, and say: **Love is the greatest thing. When we show love to others, we show them God's love.**

Hug-a-Bug

Topic: Loving others

Scripture: 1 John 4:16

Game Overview: Kids will catch a ball, stand on a heart, and feel a lot of love in the room.

☆ ☆ ☆ ☆ ☆

Supplies: Bible, masking tape, ball

Preparation: Use the masking tape to make a heart shape on the floor.

Gather children around the heart shape, and say: **God loves us so much! The Bible even tells us that God is love!** Read aloud 1 John 4:16; then continue: **Let's show one another God's love by playing Hug-a-Bug. I'll toss the ball to someone, and that person will be the "bug." The bug will take the ball and stand on the heart shape in the middle. Then the rest of us will go into the middle of the circle and hug the bug. The bug will toss the ball to someone else, who will become the new bug.**

Begin tossing the ball, and then leading children in a group hug. When everyone has had a turn to be the bug, say: **Now that we've all been hugged, let's learn a song about God's love.** Lead children in singing the following song, to the tune of "This Old Man." You may want to toss the ball around the circle while children sing. Whoever is holding the ball at the end of the song will be the center of a group hug.

> **I love God.**
> **God loves me.**
> **That's the way it ought to be!**
> **God will give me love,**
> **And I'll pass it on to you!**
> **Won't you say you love God, too?**

☆ ☆ ☆ ☆ ☆

At the end of the game, discuss the following questions:

• **How does God show his love to you?**

• **How do we show love to others?**

Tell kids to play the Hug-a-Bug game with family and friends. It's a great way to show love to others!

Protecting Moses

Topic: Moses

Scripture: Exodus 2:1-10

Game Overview: Kids will play a game in which they're reeds in the Nile River, and they'll see how God protected the baby Moses.

★ ★ ★ ★ ★

Supplies: Bible, wicker basket, doll, blanket, masking tape

Preparation: Use masking tape to make a zigzag line across the room. Wrap the doll in a blanket, and put it in a wicker basket to represent baby Moses.

Open your Bible to Exodus 2:1-10, and briefly tell the story of baby Moses floating down the Nile in a basket and being found by Pharaoh's daughter. Remind children that the river was a dangerous place where God protected baby Moses. Say: **Let's experience what it might have been like for baby Moses to float down the Nile River in a basket. Let's protect him, as God protected him.**

Ask children to stand on either side of the zigzag line so that no one is close enough to touch another person without moving. The kids will pretend to be reeds in the Nile River. First, you'll pretend to be a crocodile and walk back and forth on the tape line at a predictable pace, opening and closing your arms in rhythm like a crocodile mouth. Start the basket at one end of the river, and ask the children to push it from one person to another—pushing the baby from reed to reed, keeping him away from the crocodile. When baby Moses gets to the end of the river, have everyone shout, "Yea! God protected Moses!"

★ ★ ★ ★ ★

At the end of the game, discuss the following questions:
- **How did you protect Moses in our game?**
- **How did God protect Moses in the Bible story?**

Say: **God protected Moses all his life and God protects us, too. We'll grow up to work for God as Moses did.**

Run, Run, as fast as You can

HIGH ★★★★★★★★★ ENERGY

Topic: Moses

Scripture: Exodus 13:17–14:31

Game Overview: Kids will act out the story and run through the water away from Pharaoh's army.

★ ★ ★ ★ ★

Supplies: Bible, two long pieces of rope or yarn

Preparation: Place the rope pieces side by side in a straight line across your room.

Open your Bible to Exodus 13:17–14, and tell kids the story of Moses and the Israelites crossing the Red Sea. Show children the ropes that are side by side on the floor. Say: **God told Moses to stretch out his hand over the water to divide it.** Have four kids each grab one of the ends of the ropes, then move them apart to separate them. Then have kids move the ropes back together. Tell them they'll do that movement as you experience the story in a moment.

Teach this refrain for children to shout to the Egyptian soldiers:

Run, run, as fast as you can.

You can't catch us. We're part of God's plan.

Divide kids into two groups, and have one group be the Israelites and the other group be Pharaoh's army. You will be Moses and ask the Israelites to line up

Leader Tip

Let Moses decide which method of locomotion his people should take (hopping, skipping, and crawling are a few possibilities). Change the refrain accordingly.

behind you at one end of the ropes. Have Pharaoh's army line up behind the Israelites.

Then play the game. Hold up your hand, and have the rope holders move the ropes apart. Lead the Israelites in running between the ropes and shouting to the soldiers: "Run, run, as fast as you can. You can't catch us. We're part of God's plan." Have Pharaoh's army begin to run between the ropes, and then have the rope holders bring the ropes together and catch the army.

Let children play several times, changing roles each time.

☆ ☆ ☆ ☆ ☆

At the end of the game, discuss the following questions:
• **How did God save Moses and the Israelites in this game?**
• **What was it like for you to run through the divided waters?**
Say: **God made the waters divide so Moses and the Israelites could get away from that army! God saved his people in a mighty way that day!**

The Israelites' Journey

Topic: Moses

Scripture: Exodus

Game Overview: Kids will play a circle game and sing a song about all that happened to Moses and God's people.

☆ ☆ ☆ ☆ ☆

Supplies: Bible, masking tape

Preparation: Use masking tape to form a circle on the floor of your room. Make the circle large enough so kids can stand on it while holding hands.

Summarize the story of the Israelites wandering around the desert. Start the game by spacing the kids around the outer boundaries of your masking tape circle. Have them slowly spin their bodies as you sing this rhyme to the tune of "Ring Around the Rosie:"

> **Outside the Promised Land,**
> **The Israelites could not stand.**
> **Griping, grumbling,**
> **They all fall down.** (*Children drop to the ground.*)

Repeat this until children become familiar with the rhyme. Then have kids stand on the masking tape circle, hold hands, and march in place as you sing the next verse of the rhyme:

> **Closer to the Promised Land;**
> **Hold each other by the hand—**
> **Working together,**
> **We all jump in!** (*Children jump into the circle.*)

☆ ☆ ☆ ☆ ☆

At the end of the game, have kids sit on the masking tape circle. Discuss these questions:

• **What do you remember about the Bible story?**

• **Would you like to have been with Moses and the people while they traveled from the desert to the Promised Land? Why or why not?**

Say: **God was with his people as they traveled a long time. God is with us, too, no matter where we live or where we travel.**

Arky, Arky

Topic: Noah

Scripture: Genesis 6–9:17

Game Overview: Kids will act out the parts of the animals and of Noah and get into the ark as it starts to rain.

☆ ☆ ☆ ☆ ☆

Supplies: Bible, masking tape, spray bottle filled with water

Preparation: Use masking tape to make an ark shape on the floor in a corner of your room. Refer to the illustration above for guidance. The ark should be large enough so all children can stand inside it.

Use this game when you tell children the story of Noah and the ark (Genesis 6–9:17). Choose one child to be Noah. Have the others choose an animal sound to make. When you say, "It looks like rain," have kids wander around the room making their animal sounds and acting like the animals. Have Noah tag the animals and bring them to the ark. Stand by the ark, and lightly spray the children with water as they enter it. When all the animals are in the ark, have Noah step inside, too. When you say, "God closed the door," have all kids and Noah repeat the phrase and clap once to sound like a door closing. Ask the ark passengers to rock back and forth as they sing, "Row, Row, Row Your Boat." Then have everyone say, "Ooh! A rainbow!" Let all ark passengers get out of the ark. Finally, have Noah say, "Thanks, God, for saving us!"

Play the game several times, and have several children be Noah. At the end of the game, discuss the following questions:

• **What did you like about playing this game?**

• **What do you remember most about the story?**

Say: **God saved Noah's family and the animals. God gave us a beautiful rainbow and a promise never to flood the whole earth again.**

Leader Tip

You could make an obstacle course for the animals to travel through to get on the ark. Have kids walk along a piece of yarn for a tightrope, crawl through a table covered with a blanket for a tunnel, step on paper-circle stepping-stones for crossing a river, and crawl over a chair for a mountain.

Rainbow Ball

Topic: Noah

Scripture: Genesis 9:12-16

Game Overview: Kids will toss a beautiful ball and be reminded that God always keeps his promises.

✰ ✰ ✰ ✰ ✰

Supplies: Bible, bag of cotton batting, string, sock, tape, long strips of rainbow-colored ribbon or crepe paper

Preparation: Push a handful of cotton batting into the toe of the sock. You should have a somewhat firm ball. Tie a knot in the sock just above the batting. Use string to attach crepe paper or ribbons to the other end of the sock. Suspend the remainder of the batting from the ceiling by tying several pieces of string around it and then taping the ends of the string to the ceiling. This "cloud" should hang just a bit higher than the children's heads.

Read Genesis 9:12-16, about God setting his rainbow in the clouds as a sign of his promise. Have children stand on one side of the cloud. Show them how the ball creates a rainbow when it's thrown up and over the cloud above their heads. Each child may take a turn moving to the other side of the cloud and throwing the ball over the cloud to someone he or she selects from the group. This "catcher" becomes the "thrower" in the next round. The thrower may return to the group after his or her turn. Teach children this rhyme to repeat together each time the thrower throws:

> **Promises, promises—**
> **God always keeps his promises**
> **To Noah and to** [child's name the thrower has selected to catch the ball].

Play until each child has had a turn throwing and catching.

✰ ✰ ✰ ✰ ✰

At the end of the game, discuss the following questions:

• **What does the Bible tell us that a rainbow means?**

• **What did God promise Noah?**

Say: **The rainbow is a sign of God's promise to never flood the whole earth again. God promises to love us and care for us forever.**

Indoor Ski

Topic: Obedience

Scripture: Deuteronomy 28:1-2

Game Overview: Kids will follow the rules as they take turns being the skier and the poles in this game.

☆ ☆ ☆ ☆ ☆

Supplies: Bible, wax paper

Preparation: To play this game, find a room with carpeted floors. Tear off two two-foot lengths of wax paper for every three kids.

Ask kids to stand on one side of the room. Have them form trios and choose who will be the skier and who will be the two poles. Give each skier two skis to stand on—two lengths of wax paper! Ask the "poles" to stand on either side of the skier. Say: **Let's play a game, and you have to obey the rules! Poles, you must protect your skier as you help him or her to the other wall and back. Skiers hold onto your poles for support and shuffle your feet along on the wax paper. Don't lift your feet, just shuffle.** Quickly demonstrate. **Poles, if your skier loses a ski, take your skier back and get it again. Skiers, keep your feet on your skis and your hands on your poles at all times. Ready? Ski!**

Play the game several times, letting kids experience being the skier and the poles. Throughout the game, remind the poles to protect their skiers so the skiers don't fall and get hurt. At the end of the game, discuss the following questions:

- **Who did you obey in this game?**
- **Why did you obey?**

Read Deuteronomy 28:1-2. Ask:

- **Who else should we obey? Why?**

Say: **We obey the rules in games so everyone does what's right and nobody gets hurt. We obey God because God wants us to do what's right and not get hurt. We obey God because we love him!**

Joshua Obeys

Topic: Obedience

Scripture: Joshua 6

Game Overview: Kids will build a circular wall, march around it, knock it over, and remember how Joshua obeyed God.

✮ ✮ ✮ ✮ ✮

Supplies: Old milk cartons, small boxes, cardboard blocks, several beach balls, whistle

Preparation: Set out the supplies.

Finish the story of the walls of Jericho with a rousing round of this game. Have kids make the walls of Jericho by stacking milk cartons, boxes, or blocks side by side and several rows high in a circle. Have all the children form a circle around the wall. Say: **God told Joshua and his men to march around the walls of Jericho for six days. Let's do that now.** Lead kids in marching around the walls. Each time you get all the way around, count out, "One," "two," "three," and so on up to "six."

Have kids stop while you say: **On the seventh day, God had them march around the city again. When they heard a trumpet blast, everyone was to give a loud shout, and the wall would fall down.** Lead everyone around the wall and count out "Seven!" Blow your whistle, and have everyone shout, "Joshua obeyed God!" Then let everyone take turns tossing the beach balls at the wall to topple it over. Have kids repair the wall and play again.

✮ ✮ ✮ ✮ ✮

At the end of the game, discuss the following questions:

• **What happened when Joshua obeyed God?**

• **Why does God want us to obey him?**

Say: **Joshua obeyed God and won! The word spread all over the country about how God helped Joshua. God knows what's best for us. When we obey God, we show others how much we love God.**

Tail of a Big Fish

Topic: Obedience

Scripture: Jonah

Game Overview: Kids will play a chasing game and see why Jonah should have obeyed God.

☆ ☆ ☆ ☆ ☆

Supplies: Bible

Preparation: None needed

Ask children to stand in a line and have each child hold onto the waist of the child in front of him or her. Tell kids to pretend that they're a big fish swishing through the ocean. The person at the head of the fish will try to catch the tail by tagging the person at the back of the line. Encourage all of the children to hold on tightly as the fish twists and turns. When the "tail" is finally tagged, have the first child in line become the new tail. Have the second person in line become the new "head," and start the game again.

Have kids say this rhyme as they play:

Big fish, big fish in the sea,
You caught Jonah but you can't catch me.

Continue until each child has had a chance to be the head of the big fish.

☆ ☆ ☆ ☆ ☆

At the end of the game, discuss the following questions:

· **What did God want Jonah to do?**
· **What happened to Jonah because he didn't obey God?**

Say: **When Jonah was in the belly of the big fish, he prayed to God and said he was sorry for not obeying. God freed Jonah from the fish, and Jonah finally obeyed God. Let's obey God always!**

Path of Praises

Topic: Praising God

Scripture: Luke 19:28-38

Game Overview: Kids will praise one another, then praise God in this affirming game.

☆ ☆ ☆ ☆ ☆

Supplies: Bible

Preparation: None needed

> ## Leader Tip
> Every now and then, have kids go down the path of praises in different ways: hopping, jumping, sliding, dancing, galloping, and so on.

Make a "path" by having kids stand in two lines facing each other. Ask kids to spread out so the path extends from one end of the room to the other.

Open your Bible to Luke 19:28-38. Tell kids about all the people praising Jesus as he rode into Jerusalem. Then ask the first child in one of the lines to walk down the path they've made. As the child walks, have the other children wave their hands in the air and yell affirmations or cheers such as "Hooray" and "Yea, [child's name]!"

When the child reaches the end of the path, have the child rejoin the line. Then have the first child from the other line walk down the path. Continue until everyone has walked down the path of praises.

☆ ☆ ☆ ☆ ☆

At the end of the game, discuss the following questions:

• **How did you feel hearing all that praise?**

• **How do you think Jesus feels when we praise him?**

Say: **Jesus must feel good when we praise him. We can praise him because he is good, loving, and powerful. Let's praise Jesus now!**

Ask kids to stand in their two lines again and imagine Jesus is walking down the path. Encourage them to shout and cheer their praises to Jesus.

Overflowing Praise

Topic: Praising God

Scripture: Psalm 23:5

Game Overview: Kids will fill cups to overflowing as they praise God for many blessings.

✩ ✩ ✩ ✩ ✩

Supplies: Bible, large bowl, tarp, pitchers of water, variety of sizes of cups and measuring cups

Preparation: Set the supplies on a tarp or go outside.

R ead Psalm 23:5, and tell kids that God gives us so many good gifts, or blessings, that sometimes we say that "our cup overflows."

Have children fill up their cups with water and pour the water into the bowl until the water overflows. For every cup of water kids place in the bowl, have them each say one blessing, such as a good family or fun friends. Continue adding water and saying praises until the water overflows. Then have kids shout, "My cup overflows!"

Pour the water back into the pitchers, and let kids start over. Encourage them to count the number of cups of water they put in the bowl. See how many blessings they can praise God for!

✩ ✩ ✩ ✩ ✩

At the end of the game, discuss the following questions:

• **How many blessings did you praise God for?**

• **What was it like when the bowl overflowed with water?**

Say: **We just want to overflow or spill out all kinds of praises to God for all of his blessings. We have such a good God!**

Leader Tip

Use this game while enjoying a snack. Have each child put a cupful of various small snack items—such as chocolate chips, M&M's candy, and cereal—into a big bowl. Mix the treats together, and have each child scoop out a cupful of treats to enjoy. Our cup overflows with sweet blessings!

Guess Who's Talking

Topic: Prayer

Scripture: 2 Chronicles 30:27

Game Overview: Kids will record their voices, then listen as they learn God hears our prayers.

☆ ☆ ☆ ☆ ☆

Supplies: Bible, cassette recorder, blank tape

Preparation: Practice with the cassette recorder and blank tape to be sure it will pick up and clearly replay a speaking voice.

Gather children in an area where the tape recorder can be easily used. Say: **Each of us is going to record a message on the tape. Then we'll play the tape to see if we can guess who's talking. When it's your turn, say, "God knows my voice when I talk to him."**

Record each child's voice, and then rewind the tape to the beginning.

Ask children to find a new place in the circle, and then play the tape and let kids guess who's talking.

☆ ☆ ☆ ☆ ☆

At the end of the game, discuss the following question:

• **What do you think it's like for God to hear all of our different voices?**

Read 2 Chronicles 30:27; then say: **God doesn't have to *guess* who's talking to him. God *knows* the voice of each person who talks to him. God hears us when we pray to him!**

Leader Tip

You may want to jot down the order in which children speak. Be sure to leave a brief space after each voice so you can start and stop the tape without cutting off anyone's words.

God Is Listening

Topic: Prayer

Scripture: Proverbs 15:29

Game Overview: Kids will close their eyes and listen carefully, trying to identify objects that are dropped.

☆ ☆ ☆ ☆ ☆

Supplies: Bible; various items such as a safety pin, cotton ball, paper clip, jingle bell, facial tissue, pingpong ball, coin, pencil, crayon, chalk, plastic cup, silverware

Preparation: Gather the supplies on a hard surface such as a table.

Before the game, seat children around a table. Say: **When it's very quiet, some people say, "It was so quiet, you could've heard a pin drop." Let's hear how quiet that would be.** Have children sit quietly while you drop a safety pin on the table. **Wow! That didn't make much noise! We had to really listen to hear it.**

We're going to play a listening game. First, close your eyes tightly, and place your hands over them. Listen carefully to the sound when I drop something. See if you can guess what the object is by the sound it makes.

After children have closed their eyes and put their hands over their eyes, begin the game. Drop objects such as a jingle bell, pingpong ball, spoon, coin, and other items you've brought. Pause after each item, and allow children to guess. Then let children open their eyes to see what the item was.

☆ ☆ ☆ ☆ ☆

At the end of the game, discuss the following question:

• **How did you know what the items were?**

Say: **You needed to listen very carefully to know what made those different sounds. God listens very carefully to us, too.** Read Proverbs 15:29. **God knows each of our voices and is always ready to listen when we pray. God loves the times we talk with him. It doesn't have to be quiet for God to hear us, either. God can always hear us, whether we whisper, shout, or just talk.**

Touched by the Light

Topic: Salvation

Scripture: Matthew 4:16

Game Overview: Kids will try to save their shadows from being stepped on, then be saved by the light.

☆ ☆ ☆ ☆ ☆

Supplies: Bible, two flashlights, one lamp

Preparation: Place a bright lamp in one corner of the room. Before children arrive, test the lamp to make sure it creates clearly defined shadows when the room lights are dimmed.

Say: **Dark places can be scary—you don't know what you might trip over or run into. But usually when you shine a light into a dark place, it's not so scary after all—the darkness is gone.**

Read Matthew 4:16, and say: **When Jesus came to earth, people's hearts were dark and full of sin. But the light of Jesus shined in the dark. Jesus forgives us and saves us. It's like a light making the dark go away.**

Give two people flashlights, and tell them they're "light carriers." Turn on the lamp, and then dim the lights. Have kids look on the ground to see their shadows.

Say: **Pretend that your shadow is the sin or bad things in your heart. When I say "Go," chase one another's shadows and try to step on them. If someone steps on your shadow, freeze where you are. You must remain frozen until a light carrier shines a flashlight on your frozen shadow. When the light has touched your shadow, you're free to move again.**

☆ ☆ ☆ ☆ ☆

Stop the game every few minutes to allow children to change roles. At the end of the game, discuss these questions:

- How did the light free you so you could keep playing this game?
- How did Jesus free you from your sins?
- How can you thank Jesus for forgiving you?

Offer a prayer of thanks for Jesus' forgiveness.

A Gift for Me

Topic: Salvation

Scripture: Luke 23:26-49

Game Overview: Kids will stick bows on a cross to remind them of Jesus' gift—Jesus died for each one of them.

☆ ☆ ☆ ☆ ☆

Supplies: Bible, butcher paper, scissors, marker, masking tape, gift bows (one per child)

Preparation: Cut a 3x5-foot cross shape from butcher paper. Draw a large heart in the middle of the cross, and tape the cross to the wall at child height. Then create a line of masking tape on the floor approximately four feet away from the cross.

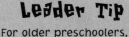

Leader Tip

For older preschoolers, blindfold them and turn them in three circles before they walk toward the cross.

Open your Bible to Luke 23:26-49, and tell kids about the beautiful gift of Jesus dying for our sins.

Write each child's name on a gift bow, and distribute the bows, one bow per child. One at a time, have each child stand behind the line, close his or her eyes, walk forward to the cross, and try to stick the bow on the cross. Encourage kids to aim for the heart on the cross, and remind them not to peek!

When each child has had a turn attaching a bow to the cross, encourage kids to take turns hopping to the cross and removing their bows. Have children hop back to the starting line, put the bows on their shirts, and say, "Jesus gave a gift to me!"

☆ ☆ ☆ ☆ ☆

At the end of the game, discuss these questions:

• **What gift did Jesus give to each one of us?**

• **How do we know Jesus loves us?**

Say: **Jesus died on the cross so that we could live forever in heaven with God—that's the greatest gift of all!**

Lost and Found

Topic: Salvation

Scripture: Luke 4:14-21

Game Overview: Kids will search for lost items as they learn that Jesus came to seek and save us all.

☆ ☆ ☆ ☆ ☆

Supplies: Bible, blanket, and familiar items such as a small ball, cross, small Bible, toy car, doll, and book about Jesus

Preparation: Place all the items on the blanket.

Open a Bible to Luke 4:14-21, and say: **Jesus said that God doesn't want anyone to be lost—God wants us all to know Jesus!**

Bring out the blanket with all the items on it. Ask kids to tell you the names of the items, and then have children close their eyes. Choose one child to take something from the blanket and hide it. Then ask the others to open their eyes, figure out what's missing, and look for the lost item.

☆ ☆ ☆ ☆ ☆

Play the game several times, and rejoice with the children over each item they find. At the end of the game, discuss these questions:

• **How did you feel when you found each lost item?**

• **How do you think God feels when one of his lost children is found?**

Say: **Jesus came for us all, to seek and save what was lost, just as you had to look for and "save" each lost item.**

Canned Food Stuff

Topic: Serving
Scripture: Colossians 3:23-24
Game Overview: Kids will race to organize canned goods.

☆ ☆ ☆ ☆ ☆

Supplies: Bible, canned goods, grocery bags or boxes, pencil
Preparation: Set the empty boxes or grocery bags close to canned goods your church has collected to give to people who need them.

> ## Leader Tip
> Depending on the amount of cans your church has collected, you might have to vary the game. Just play long enough so kids know they're helping serve others by organizing the cans.

Play this game after your church has had a canned food drive. Have kids sit in a circle, cross-legged and one foot apart. Place a pencil in the center of the circle. Show kids the canned goods and the empty containers.

Say: **We're going to play a fun game and stuff the canned goods in bags at the same time. I'll gently spin the pencil like this.** Demonstrate. **When the pencil stops spinning and points at you, you're "It"! You'll run as fast as you can to the canned goods, pick up two, place them in the bag, then run to the center of the circle. Then it's your turn to spin the pencil and find the next "It."**

Play the game, and have fun stuffing the bags! If the pencil points to someone who's already had a turn, spin the pencil again.

Play the game until kids have stuffed the cans in the containers. Read aloud Colossians 3:23-24, and then ask the following question:

• **What does God want us to do? Why?**

Say: **When we serve others, we're also serving God!**

cleaning crew

Topic: Serving

Scripture: John 13:1-17

Game Overview: Kids will serve the church by cleaning, then they'll play a game with water.

★ ★ ★ ★ ☆

Supplies: Bible, rags (one for every child), buckets of soapy water and buckets of clean water (for every four children)

Preparation: Find floors around your church that kids can clean, such as the nursery, kitchen, or bathrooms.

Read John 13:1-17, and tell kids about Jesus showing ultimate servanthood when he washed his disciples' feet. Then gather the kids on one of the floors you've arranged for them to clean. Set out the cleaning supplies, and play a game with the servants. Have kids form two teams, and assign each team half of the floor to clean. When a team finishes, its members will help the other team clean. Then go to the next floor you've arranged for kids to clean. Mix the kids and form two new teams. Assign each team half of the floor to clean, and play the game again. Remind children to watch for slippery floors as they work.

★ ★ ★ ★ ☆

After the cleaning games, discuss these questions:

• **What do you feel like after you've helped someone?**

• **Why does Jesus want us to serve others?**

Say: **Jesus showed us how to serve, so we can serve others too. When we serve others, we show them Jesus' love.**

Take kids outside to play a refreshing water game. Form teams of four, and place a bucket of clean water in the middle of each team. Ask the kids to take off their shoes and socks.

Say: **Let's play a game and clean ourselves a bit, too! The object of this game is to see which team can empty its bucket first by using feet only. You can't lift the bucket or tip it over. Take turns stomping in the bucket to splash out the water. Ready? Go!**

Serving Others

Topic: Serving

Scripture: Mark 9:41

Game Overview: Kids will serve others, then say a rhyme as they wiggle their feet.

✮ ✮ ✮ ✮ ✮

Supplies: Bible, cups of cold water (one for each child)

Preparation: Arrange to have your children give cups of cold water to people in your church.

Gather the children, and read aloud Mark 9:41. Say: **Jesus loves it when we serve others—even when we give a cup of water in Jesus' name.**

Give each child a cup of water, and lead them into another area in the church so they can serve others. As kids give away their cups, have them tell the person, "Jesus loves you."

Gather everyone back and teach this song. Ask children to sit in a tight circle with their legs extended in front of them. Sing this song to the tune of "When Johnny Comes Marching Home."

God gave me feet to walk and run. *(Wave feet back and forth to the beat.)*
Hooray! *(Lift up right foot.)*
Hooray! *(Lift up left foot.)*
God gave me feet to walk and run. *(Wave feet back and forth to the beat.)*
Hooray! *(Lift up right foot.)*
Hooray! *(Lift up left foot.)*
I'll march along *(bend right knee and put foot flat)*
And sing this song. *(Bend left knee and put foot flat.)*
I'll tell of God's love *(straighten right leg)*
All day long. *(Straighten left leg.)*
And my feet will help me *(wave your feet back and forth to the beat)*
To serve the Lord each day. *(Wave your feet back and forth to the beat.)*

Sharing Shirts

Topic: Sharing

Scripture: Luke 3:11

Game Overview: Kids will play a game with shirts and learn how important it is to live for God by sharing with others.

☆ ☆ ☆ ☆ ☆

Supplies: Bible, adult-sized jackets or front-button shirts (one for every two children), CD player, praise music

Preparation: Place all the jackets in a pile on the floor.

Gather kids in a circle around the pile of jackets. Tell about John the Baptist's message to share clothes with people who didn't have any (Luke 3:11).

Say: **Let's play a fun game to help us learn that God wants us to share. While the music plays, see how fast you can put on a jacket, take it off, and pass it on. When the music stops, everyone freeze!**

Start the music, and have kids find a jacket, put it on, take it off, and pass it along. Stop the music and have kids freeze. Some will have jackets and some won't. Ask:

• **How can you share your jackets?**

Have kids fit two per jacket. Play music while the pairs dance in their shared shirts. Stop the music and have kids freeze.

Ask kids to take off the jackets and place them in the center of the circle. Take out two or three shirts, and say: **Now, there really aren't enough shirts for everyone. How can you share?**

Play the music, and have kids try to fit three children in each shirt. Stop the music and have kids freeze.

☆ ☆ ☆ ☆ ☆

At the end of the game, discuss the following questions:

• **How did those of you who didn't have a jacket feel?**

• **How did it feel to share with someone?**

Say: **God wants us to share with others. When we share with others, we show people God's love.**

Believers' Belongings

Topic: Sharing

Scripture: Acts 2:42-47

Game Overview: Kids will get firsthand practice sharing toys in this game.

☆ ☆ ☆ ☆ ☆

Supplies: Bible, toys (one per child), CD player, contemporary Christian music

Preparation: Place the toys in the center of your room.

Ask children to sit in a circle around the toys. Play the music, and pass the toys around the circle to the beat. Stop the music, and have kids each play with the toy that's in their hands.

After kids have played for about one minute, read Acts 2:42-47. Say: **The people in the very first church shared what they had with each other. We can share too! Friends share their toys, their food, and their fun. Let's practice sharing right now. You might really like the toy you're playing with now, but let's switch and share.**

Play the music again, and have kids again pass the toys in the circle. Stop the music, and have kids each play with the new toy that's in their hands. Have the children all say, "Thank you for sharing" to kids on both sides of them.

Continue playing as long as time allows.

☆ ☆ ☆ ☆ ☆

At the end of the game, discuss the following questions:

• **How did you like sharing in this game?**

• **Why does Jesus want us to share?**

• **Who can you share with when you go home?**

Say: **Let's remember to share our toys, food, and fun with family and friends. Jesus wants us to love one another and share what we have.**

> ## Leader Tip
>
> For added fun, have children pass the toys in opposite directions with their eyes closed or as quickly as possible. You could also take out a few toys every time, and have kids with toys share with the kids who have no toys.

Look Up

Topic: Thankfulness

Scripture: Psalm 136:1

Game Overview: Kids will look for God's treasures in all directions.

☆ ☆ ☆ ☆ ☆

Leader Tip

Take kids outside for an "I'm So Thankful Search." Have them look up, look down, and look all around for things they want to thank God for.

Supplies: Bible, yarn, tape, treats

Preparation: Tie long pieces of yarn to treats. You'll need enough treats for each child to have one. Tape the yarn to the ceiling so the treats hang above kids' heads, high enough so they'll have to stretch to reach them.

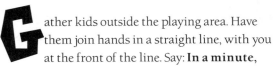ather kids outside the playing area. Have them join hands in a straight line, with you at the front of the line. Say: **In a minute, I'll have you close your eyes and I'll lead you into the room. When you're all in the room, I'll tell you which direction to look. Then open your eyes, and hunt for good gifts in that direction. Then I'll tell you another direction to look. Don't look anywhere until I tell you to!**

Lead the kids inside the room, and say: **Before you open your eyes, put your chin on your chest.** Pause while kids do this. **Keep your chin in this position so when you open your eyes, you'll be looking only on the ground. Ready? Keep your chin on your chest, open your eyes, and look on the ground. Tell me what good gifts you see in this direction.** Kids might name gifts such as carpet, chairs, shoes, and so on.

Say: **Keep your chin on your chest, and look at the ground until I tell you another direction to look! Place your hands above your eyes, and look straight ahead of you. What gifts do you see in this direction?** Kids might name each other, pictures on the wall, tables, and bookshelves.

Say: **Keep holding your hands above your eyes until I tell you another direction to look! On the count of three, take your hands down then look up. Ready? One, two, three!** Kids will see the treats taped to the ceiling. Help them get the treats, and let kids enjoy them.

☆ ☆ ☆ ☆ ☆

At the end of the game, discuss the following questions:

· **Where did you look to find the gifts?**

· **What do you like about the gifts?**

· **How can you thank God for all the gifts he gives you?**

Say: **Just like these treats are good, God is *so* good. We can look up** (have kids do this), **look down** (have kids do this), **and look all around** (have kids do this) **to see so many gifts God gives us.** Read Psalm 136:1. **Let's remember to always thank God for his good gifts.**

Go around the room and have children say things they see that they're thankful for.

Stackin' and Snackin'

Topic: Thankfulness

Scripture: 1 Chronicles 16:34

Game Overview: Kids will stack a snack and say all kinds of things they're thankful for.

☆ ☆ ☆ ☆ ☆

Supplies: Bible, cookies, canned frosting, paper plates, cookie sheet, craft sticks

Preparation: Set the supplies on a table.

Encourage kids to wash their hands before this game. Have kids form trios, and hand each trio a paper plate.

Say: **When I say, "Stack 'em high," take turns frosting a cookie and stacking cookies on top of one another on your plate. Each time you stack a cookie, say something you're thankful for. Ready? Stack 'em high!**

After four minutes, see how high kids have stacked 'em.

☆ ☆ ☆ ☆ ☆

Combine cookie stacks on the cookie sheet, and then discuss the following questions:

- **What are you thankful for?**
- **How do you give God thanks?**

Read 1 Chronicles 16:34, and say: **We should give God thanks for he is good and he loves us forever. Look at this stack of thanksgivings! I'm so thankful for all God's given us.**

Let everyone help gobble down the goodies!

> ## Leader Tip
>
> For older preschoolers, you could have kids stack the cookies relay-style. Have them stand twenty feet away from the table of supplies, hop to the table, frost and stack a cookie, shout out a thanksgiving, and race back.

A Stormy Sea

Topic: Trust

Scripture: Matthew 14:22-33

Game Overview: Kids will see what floats and what sinks in water.

☆ ☆ ☆ ☆ ☆

Supplies: Bible; child's plastic wading pool; towels; a tarp (if you're playing inside); and objects that sink or float such as plastic tubs, pingpong balls, beach balls, and blocks

Preparation: Fill the pool half-full of water. Set the towels and objects around it.

Ask kids to take off their shoes and socks and roll up their pants. Then gather kids around the pool. Say: **Let's all step in the pool and see how good it feels.** Let everyone step in and say "Ah-h-h." **Who thinks they can walk on top of the water?** Let kids try. **Nobody can walk on top of the water, but Jesus can! Peter walked for a while on water when he kept looking at Jesus and trusting him! Let's hear about Peter and Jesus walking on the water.**

Have everyone step out of the pool and dry off their feet as you read Matthew 14:22-33 to them. Say: **When Peter trusted Jesus, he could walk on water.** Place a floatable object on the water. **When he looked away and saw the stormy sea, he got scared and sank.** Place a sinkable object in the water. **Let's see what else sinks or floats.** Let kids play with the other objects to discover what sinks or floats.

☆ ☆ ☆ ☆ ☆

At the end of the game, discuss the following questions:

• **What do you remember about Jesus in our Bible story?** Place a floatable object in the pool, and have kids pass it from person to person as they say what they remember.

• **When have you been scared, like Peter?** Place a sinkable object in the water, and have kids pass it from person to person as they share a fear.

Say: **We need to trust Jesus to take care of us when we're scared. Jesus loves us and gives us family and friends to take care of us. We can always trust Jesus.**

It's Stickin'

HIGH ENERGY

Topic: Trust

Scripture: Hebrews 13:5b-6a

Game Overview: Kids will play a game with clothespins and know that God never leaves them.

☆ ☆ ☆ ☆ ☆

Supplies: Bible, clothespins, 3x5 cards (one for each child), marker

Preparation: Use a marker to write "God" on each clothespin. Gather the supplies.

Ask kids to sit in a circle, and give each child a 3x5 card. Instruct children to place the cards on their shoulders. Say: **Now, see if you can shake the card off your shoulder, without using your hands.** When children have tried this, say: **That was too easy. Let's make this game a little more challenging!**

Clip a clothespin to each child's back, close enough to children's shoulders so they can feel and see them, but not where they can easily reach the clothespins. When each child is "wearing" a clothespin, say: **Now, try to shake off these clothespins, without using your hands.** Allow children to jump, hop, shake, and move about as they try to loosen the clothespins. (They'll have a great time trying!) After a minute, gather children and ask:

• **Which was easier to lose, the card or the clothespin? Why?**

☆ ☆ ☆ ☆ ☆

Read aloud Hebrews 13:5b-6a; then say: **The Bible teaches us that we can trust God to always be with us. God never leaves us. God never walks away. God isn't like the card—something that easily falls away. Instead, God is more like the clothespin. We can trust God to stay with us wherever we go.** Ask:

• **How do you feel, knowing that God will never leave you?**

• **When might be a good time to trust that God is with you?**

Let children wear their clothespins home as reminders that God never leaves us.

Leader Tip

If you have older preschoolers, you may want to ask how they knew that the clothespins were on their backs. Help children understand that, even though we can't *see* God, we can trust that he's always there.

Early Elementary Games

Jesus said, "Whoever humbles himself like this child is the greatest in the kingdom of heaven" (Matthew 18:4). Jesus held up a child as the example. Children are bright, inquisitive, quick to laugh, and simply fun to be around.

Use the games in this section to encourage and affirm the "greatest in the kingdom"! The fun games in this book are noncompetitive because there are no losers in the kingdom of heaven! The discussion questions in the games help early elementary kids connect to real-life issues such as friendship, choices, God's love, prayer, school, and living as the body of Christ.

feed Your friends

Topic: The Bible
Scripture: Matthew 14:13-21
Game Overview: Kids will feed and be fed by their teammates.

☆ ☆ ☆ ☆ ☆

Supplies: Bible, toothpicks, paper cupcake-pan liners, candy corn
Preparation: None needed

Form teams of four kids each. Ask each team to sit in a line. Give each person a toothpick and a paper cupcake-pan liner with four pieces of candy corn in it. Say: **Let's feed our friends! You can't touch the candy with your hands, and you can't eat directly out of your cup. Another team member must feed you. The first person in line will feed all four pieces of candy to the player behind him or her. Pierce the candy with the toothpick, and place it in the other person's mouth. Then the person you've fed will feed the person behind him or her, and so on. The last person should then jump up, run to the front of the line, and feed the first person. Ready? Feed your friends!**

Time the races, and have kids play again. Hand out more candy corn, and see whether players can beat their time.

Gather kids in a circle, and read Matthew 14:13-21 to them. Then discuss the following questions:

· **What was it like to feed your friends in this relay? to be fed?**
· **What do you think it was like for Jesus to feed the crowd?**

• What other Bible stories do you know that tell us of feeding the hungry?

Say: **It was fun to feed our friends in the relay. I was amazed at how you could do it with just those toothpicks! The crowd of 5,000 must have been amazed when Jesus fed all the people that day. God's Word feeds us with stories of how much he loves us and takes care of us. Let's fill up on God's Word each day!**

Leader Tip

Use this game to introduce any Bible story that has food in it: Exodus 16; Matthew 15:29-39; or Mark 6:32-44.

Brick Fortress

Topic: The Bible

Scripture: 2 Samuel 22:2-3

Game Overview: Kids will use edible bricks to build a mighty fortress.

☆ ☆ ☆ ☆ ☆

Supplies: Bible, mini-cakes, icing, plastic knives, tablecloth

Preparation: Organize families or church volunteers who have petite loaf pans to bake your bricks. Then invite the brick bakers to your class to watch kids build the mightiest fortress. Afterward, everyone can enjoy eating the masterpiece! Lay out a tablecloth, and set the building supplies on it.

> ### Leader Tip
>
> One cake mix makes 16 mini-cakes. You'll need about 1½ cups of icing for every 16 mini-cakes. If you don't want to have people bake cake bricks for the building project, you could purchase Hostess cupcakes for kids to "ice" together.

Read any Scripture that tells of God being a mighty fortress, for example, 2 Samuel 22:2-3. Tell kids that a mighty fortress is like a castle or a strong building that people would run to for protection. Motion toward the supplies and tell kids they get to work together to build the mightiest fortress.

Ask kids in the "construction crew" to wash their hands. Then give them the supplies, and let them go to work building and mortaring the structure.

When kids have completed the fortress, have the volunteer bakers and the builders surround it so you can take a picture to preserve this moment in history.

☆ ☆ ☆ ☆ ☆

> ### Leader Tip
>
> Psalms is full of other "fortress" Scriptures, such as 18:2; 31:2-3; and 71:3.

As you eat the masterpiece, discuss the following questions:

• **What did you like about building your fortress?**

• **What do you think a real fortress is like?**

• **How is God our fortress?**

Say: **The Bible tells us in 2 Samuel 22:2-3 that God is our fortress. God protects us and loves us always. Run to God when you have a problem, and trust he'll protect you.**

Bible Pairs

Topic: The Bible

Scripture: Any Scripture about Bible pairs such as Genesis 2 (Adam and Eve), Genesis 4 (Cain and Abel), and 1 Samuel 17 (David and Goliath)

Game Overview: Kids will guess identities as they review the Bible.

☆ ☆ ☆ ☆ ☆

Supplies: Bibles, paper, markers, tape, name tags, chalk, chalkboard

Preparation: Set out the supplies.

Start out by having kids brainstorm for various favorite Bible pairs such as David and Goliath, Cain and Abel, Adam and Eve, and Jacob and Esau. Have kids share whether the characters are from the Old or New Testament, good guys or bad guys, and some basic events of their lives. Write the names on the board, and leave them for all to see during the game.

Write each Bible name on a separate sheet of paper. Then tape one sheet on each child's back so he or she can't see it. Give each child a name tag to wear in front.

Tell kids the object of this game is to ask questions that can be answered yes or no to find out which Bible characters are written on their backs. After they've guessed their characters, they have to find their partners, too. So if a child has "David" written on his or her back, the child would find "Goliath," say, "Howdy, partner," and shake hands. If Goliath hasn't figured out who he or she is yet, Goliath can guess correctly after he sees "David" written on the partner's back.

Kids also must use the real names of the people they're speaking to each time they ask a question. For example, "Kristin, am I from the New Testament?" If a person forgets to use a real name, kids won't answer the question. If someone doesn't know the answer to a question, it's OK to say so.

☆ ☆ ☆ ☆ ☆

At the end of the game, discuss the following questions:
• **What's one lesson the Bible person on your back has taught you?**
• **Why should we learn about people in the Bible?**

Say: **When we learn about people in the Bible, we know how they relied on God and learned from their mistakes as well as their successes. God gives us the Bible to guide us.**

Blink of an Eye

Topic: Body of Christ

Scripture: 1 Corinthians 12:27

Game Overview: Kids will learn new things about one another and "freeze" as the lights go off and on.

☆ ☆ ☆ ☆ ☆

Supplies: Bible

Preparation: None needed

Say: **In this game, whenever you see the lights flash off and on, you must freeze wherever you are. I'll tell you what to do when everyone is frozen. Right now, find a partner, shake your partner's hand, and say one thing you like to do, such as read or play games.**

After one minute, flash the lights off and on and kids will freeze.

Say: **Next, find two people, join hands, and tell one another one thing you can do well, such as play soccer or cheer people up. Ready? Go!**

Continue to flash lights off and on at various times. Say these things:

• **Form a circle with three more people, and give a group hug.**

• **Shake three people's hands and say, "Hi, I'm [your name]."**

• **Put your arm around someone's shoulders and say the name of someone you love.**

• **Lean against the wall and shout out one thing you like to do on Saturday mornings.**

• **Sit cross-legged in one large circle and take a deep breath.**

☆ ☆ ☆ ☆ ☆

At the end of the game, discuss the following questions:

• **What new things did you learn about people in this game?**

• **How are we alike? different?**

Read 1 Corinthians 12:27. Go around the circle and say each person's name; then say: **God made each one of us special.** Have everyone link arms. **But all together we are the body of Christ. Each one of us is a part of it.**

Weave a Basket

Topic: Body of Christ
Scripture: Romans 12:5
Game Overview: Kids will complete a race after they've entwined themselves together.

★ ★ ★ ★ ★

Supplies: Bible, plastic flagging tape
Preparation: You'll need three rolls of plastic flagging tape for each team of six to eight children. (Flagging tape is the brightly colored plastic rolls of tape that construction workers use to seal off an area. You can find the tape in most hardware stores for a very reasonable price.) You'll also need a helper for each team.

Form teams of six to eight children. Have each team sit in a circle on the floor with children's feet touching in the center. Ask children to raise their hands straight above their heads.

Ask the helpers to weave the flagging tape around each child as they'd weave a basket. Weave their bodies and arms together. Use all three rolls of tape with each team. Tie the ends to the "baskets" so the baskets don't come undone.

Ask the baskets to stand up. Read Romans 12:5, and say: **We who are many, form one part. We are the body of Christ.**

Designate start and finish lines, and have the baskets run a race. Or have them rotate in a clockwise direction as they move around the room. Call the

groups back and have them sit down, still woven together. Have kids take off the plastic strips and place them in a pile in the center of the circle. Discuss the following questions:

• **What was it like to be together in this game?**

• **What does the Bible mean about being part of the body of Christ?**

Say: **Although each one of us is a special person, we work together to tell others about Jesus' love. We are the body of Christ.**

Rockin' On

Topic: Body of Christ

Scripture: 1 Corinthians 12:12

Game Overview: Kids will find rocks, get rid of them, and then try to find the same rocks they originally had.

☆ ☆ ☆ ☆ ☆

Supplies: Bible, rocks, marker, blindfolds

Preparation: If there are no rocks around your church, bring potatoes for kids to use instead.

Go outside for a walk around the church. Have each child find one rock to hold in the palm of his or her hand. Lead kids back inside, and have them sit in a circle. Give kids two minutes to touch their rocks and become familiar with them.

Then collect each rock, and use a marker to write the owner's initials on it. Ask you collect each rock, have the child say one thing about himself or herself that is unique or special, such as, "I can do a cartwheel" or "I can place my fingers in my mouth and whistle." Put the rocks in the center of the circle.

Say: **Today we're going to learn that God doesn't make any copies. Each thing God makes is unique and special. In a minute, I'll blindfold you and pass around the rocks. Your job is to determine which rock is yours.**

Blindfold the kids, and pass each rock around the circle. As children decide which rocks are theirs, have them keep them. After everyone has a rock, have children remove their blindfolds. Ask them to look at the initials to determine whether the rocks they're holding are really theirs. Have kids trade to get back their rocks if they're holding the wrong ones.

☆ ☆ ☆ ☆ ☆

At the end of the game, discuss the following questions:

- **What was unique about your rock?**
- **What about you is unique?**

Say: **God made each one of us special and one of a kind, yet together we are the body of Christ.** Have kids place their rocks in a cross shape on the floor. Read 1 Corinthians 12:12 to close.

Flash Box

Topic: Choices

Scripture: Matthew 5:15-16

Game Overview: Kids will choose which box a person is hiding under.

★ ★ ★ ★ ☆

Supplies: Bible, flashlight, three appliance boxes that a child can hide under

Preparation: Gather the supplies.

Choose a volunteer to be the "boxee," and give him or her the flashlight. Have the rest of the group face away from the boxes while the volunteer hides under one of the boxes. Help the child get under the box if necessary. Tell the child that when you say, "Let your light shine," he or she should take off the box, stand, and turn on the flashlight.

Ask the rest of the class to guess which box the volunteer chose to hide under. Tell kids to stand by the box they think the boxee has hidden under. Then say, "Let your light shine," and have the boxee stand, come out from under the box, and shine the light for all to see.

★ ★ ★ ★ ☆

Play several rounds. At the end of the game, discuss the following questions:

• **What choices did you make in this game?**

• **What choices do you make each day?**

Read aloud Matthew 5:15-16; then ask:

• **What does it mean to let our lights shine?**

• **How do you choose to let your light shine today?**

Say: **Shining our lights means telling people about Jesus' love and showing Jesus' love through our actions.**

Hey, I'm A...

Topic: Choices

Scripture: Joshua 24:15

Game Overview: Kids will choose to act out various animals and learn about choices in life.

☆ ☆ ☆ ☆ ☆

Supplies: Bible, masking tape

Preparation: Create two masking tape lines on the floor, twenty-five feet apart.

Welcome kids, and have them form two teams. Have teams line up behind one of the lines. Tell kids that when you call out two animals, kids must choose which of the two animals to move and sound like as they run the race to the opposite line and back. Then they'll tag the next team members who will run to the opposite line and back.

Call out these ideas when a runner leaves the start:

• **A duck or a dog**

• **An elephant or a kangaroo**

• **A pig or a horse**

• **A cat or a rat**

After everyone has run the race, play again and have kids choose how to act out the following things you'll call out:

• **A duck with a sore foot**

• **A little dog being chased by a big dog**

• **A monkey trying to reach a banana high in a tree**

• **A pig waddling in a mud puddle**

• **A chicken getting its feathers plucked**

☆ ☆ ☆ ☆ ☆

Gather the kids and read Joshua 24:15. Discuss the following questions:

• **What choices did you make in this game?**

• **What choices do you make each day?**

Say: **The Bible says to choose who you will serve. Joshua said, "As for me and my household, we will serve the Lord."** Go around the circle and have kids each say, "I choose to serve the Lord."

We're Coming!

Topic: Come to Jesus
Scripture: Mark 10:14
Game Overview: Kids will race under a hose or rope to come to Jesus.

☆ ☆ ☆ ☆ ☆

Supplies: Bible, one fifty-foot garden hose or rope, chair
Preparation: Fasten together the ends of the hose or rope, and lay it in a circle. Place a chair in the center of the circle.

Choose one volunteer to be the "disciple," and have the disciple stand inside the circle. Have the remaining kids gather around the outside of the circle.

Say: **Some children wanted to see Jesus. But Jesus' friends, the disciples, didn't want the children to bother Jesus. Imagine Jesus is inside this circle** (indicate the chair), **and you want to reach him. When I say "Go," lift up the hose and try to sneak under it. The disciple will try to touch you before you get through. If you're tagged, you must sit down where you were tagged. You can be freed when someone else touches you. When you touch the chair, run back outside the circle. Ready? Go!**

☆ ☆ ☆ ☆ ☆

Choose a new disciple after a minute or two, and begin a new round. At the end of the game, discuss the following questions:

• How did you feel as you tried to get into the circle?

• How did it feel when someone helped you get to "Jesus"?

Say: **Jesus wants you to come to him.** Read Mark 10:14; then ask:

• How can you come to Jesus?

Say: **You can go to church, listen to Bible stories, sing, and pray to Jesus. Come to Jesus wherever you need to and all the time. He's always there for you!**

Hear the Voice

Topic: Come to Jesus

Scripture: Matthew 11:28

Game Overview: Kids will close their eyes and follow a voice.

✰ ✰ ✰ ✰ ✰

Supplies: Bible

Preparation: None needed

Place one child in the center of the room, and tell this child to keep his or her eyes open. Ask other kids to scatter throughout the room and close their eyes.

The child whose eyes are open will silently move somewhere else in the room, then say aloud, "Come to me." Other children, with their eyes still closed, will move toward the voice until they reach the speaker as the speaker continues to say, "Come to me" every few seconds.

When kids find the speaker, they may open their eyes, then sit down and "rest" until everyone has found the speaker.

✰ ✰ ✰ ✰ ✰

At the end of the game, discuss the following questions:

• **How did it feel to rely on something other than your sight when moving toward a goal?**

• **What did you do when you reached the speaker?**

Read aloud Matthew 11:28; then ask:

• **According to this verse, who should we come to?**

• **What should we give Jesus? What will Jesus give us?**

Say: **Jesus wants us to come to him with any problems or fears or worries we have. He loves us and cares for us. Jesus will give us rest!**

Hey, Zack!

Topic: Come to Jesus

Scripture: Luke 19:1-9

Game Overview: Kids will play a game with cotton balls and imagine what it was like for Zacchaeus to come to Jesus.

✫ ✫ ✫ ✫ ✫

Supplies: Bible, artificial Christmas tree, cotton balls

Preparation: Set the tree up in your room. Place the cotton balls close to the tree.

Use this game before you tell the story of how Zacchaeus tried to see Jesus. Form groups of six kids, and give each child several cotton balls. Ask kids to form a circle around the tree, then take three steps away from it.

Tell kids they'll take turns trying to toss the cotton balls so they stick to the top of the tree. Play for a while, and let kids have several attempts.

✫ ✫ ✫ ✫ ✫

At the end of the game, compliment kids on all the cotton balls they've launched into the upper branches. Then discuss the following questions:

• **How easy or hard was it to get a cotton ball on the top of the tree?**

• **Have you ever climbed a tree? If so, was it easy or hard for you?**

Read the story of Zacchaeus in Luke 19:1-9. Then, ask:

• **How easy or hard do you think it was for Zacchaeus to climb a tree? Why?**

• **What did Jesus want Zacchaeus to do?**

Say: **Zacchaeus wanted to see Jesus so badly that he climbed a tree to do it! Jesus wanted Zacchaeus to come to him and believe in him. Jesus wants us to come to him too.**

Heels-to-Toes Race

Topic: Cooperation

Scripture: Ephesians 4:2-3

Game Overview: Kids will learn to "stick together" in this game of balance.

☆ ☆ ☆ ☆ ☆

Supplies: Bible

Preparation: None needed

Have kids form pairs and stand at one end of a hall or classroom. Ask partners to stand one behind the other, facing front to back. The child facing the partner's back must touch his or her toes to the heels of the partner at all times. To help with balance, the partner standing behind might want to hold the other partner's waist or shoulders.

When you say "Go," partners will carefully race to the other side of the room. If they break the heels-to-toes connection, partners won't start over. Just celebrate the number of steps taken, and encourage players to develop a strategy for staying together. When the

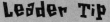

Leader Tip

Instead of pairs, have trios stand heels to toes and try to run the race. Keep adding kids until everyone is standing heels to toes and racing as one big group.

partners reach the other side of the room, they'll switch positions and return to the start line. Clap for a good job of cooperating with each other!

☆ ☆ ☆ ☆ ☆

At the end of the game, gather the kids, and read Ephesians 4:2-3. Then ask the following questions:

- **How did you work with your partner in this game?**
- **How does the Bible say we should get along?**

Ask all kids to hook up one more time, heel to toe, and say: **Make every effort to work together and get along. Jesus wants us to!**

Harvest Ride

Topic: Cooperation

Scripture: Matthew 9:37-38

Game Overview: Kids will work together to pull team members in a race.

☆ ☆ ☆ ☆ ☆

Supplies: Bible, refrigerator box

Preparation: Make four "harvest wagons" by cutting four pieces from a refrigerator box. Make a few extras in case some cardboard wagons are torn up during the game.

Have kids form four teams, and give each team a cardboard "harvest wagon." Read Matthew 9:37-38, and tell kids they're going to bring one another to the harvest field! They'll pull one another on the harvest wagons as they race to tell others about Jesus.

Have the person wearing the most white be the first harvest worker to ride the wagon while the remaining kids pull it. Have each harvest worker sit in the middle of a cardboard wagon as the others grab its front and sides.

Say: **Work together to pull your wagon across the room and back. When you reach the start line again, think of one thing you could tell people about Jesus, then shout it together. For example, "Jesus loves you!" Then pull another harvest worker, and shout another thing about Jesus. Switch riders until everyone has had a turn. Ready? Ride!**

☆ ☆ ☆ ☆ ☆

At the end of the game, discuss the following questions:

· **How did your team work together in this game?**

· **Why does God want us to work with fellow Christians?**

· **How can we work together to tell people about Jesus?**

Say: **Let's always work together to tell people that Jesus loves them!**

Grow for the Gold!

Topic: Cooperation
Scripture: Philippians 3:14
Game Overview: Kids will work together to stretch and reach a goal.

☆ ☆ ☆ ☆ ☆

Supplies: Bible, masking tape, gold-foil-wrapped Hershey's Kisses
Preparation: Create a ten-foot line on the floor with masking tape. Place the candy about thirty feet from the line.

Ask kids to stand in a line behind the masking tape. Say: **We're going to work together to reach our goal—the beautiful gold-wrapped candy. You need to hook onto one another and form a giant chain to reach the goodies. Each of you will hold the hand of another teammate until you're all holding hands. Stay standing as you hook up, but really *stretch!* The last person in line needs to keep his or her feet on the starting line at all times. If the candy is still out of reach when you're all standing and holding hands, you may have to think of other ways to stretch the line. For example, you could lie down and hold onto one another's hands and feet. Ready? Let's hook up!**

☆ ☆ ☆ ☆ ☆

After kids have worked together and reached the candy, have them celebrate by sharing and eating the treats. Read Philippians 3:14; then discuss the following questions:

- **How did you work together to reach your goal?**
- **What goal do we have as Christians?**
- **How can we work together as we stretch to reach that goal?**

Say: **We can pray for one another and encourage one another to tell people about eternal life with Jesus. What a sweet treat that will be!**

Leader Tip

You may need to vary the distance of the candy from the line, depending on the number of kids in your group. If necessary, you could form two groups that reach for two different bags.

Safe and Dry

Topic: Courage

Scripture: Joshua 1:9

Game Overview: Kids will experience the protection of umbrellas.

☆ ☆ ☆ ☆ ☆

Supplies: Bible, child-safe umbrellas, water balloons

Preparation: Fill water balloons with water, and find an area outside to play this game.

Leader Tip

Ask the kids holding umbrellas to stand far apart from one another. Warn them to be careful to keep the umbrellas away from one another's faces.

Lead kids outdoors, and have them form two groups. Give each member of one group a water balloon, and give each member of the other group an umbrella. Separate the groups by about twenty feet.

Say: **The team members with the water balloons will try to get the other team wet. The other team will use their umbrellas to try to avoid getting wet. Nobody can move any closer together. Have courage, umbrella holders! The umbrellas will protect you!**

Have teams begin. When half of the water balloons have been thrown, have teams switch roles. When everyone is in position, say to the new umbrella holders: **This time you don't get to have your umbrellas to protect you.** Wait for a few groans, and then say: **Just kidding. Have courage! You can use the umbrellas, and they'll protect you!**

☆ ☆ ☆ ☆ ☆

Gather kids and read aloud Joshua 1:9. Then discuss the following questions:

• **What was it like to have an umbrella to protect you?**

• **When do you need to have courage in real life?**

• **How does knowing God is always with you give you courage to face tough times?**

Hold an umbrella over your head, and say: **No matter what water balloons—I mean problems—come your way, have courage! Don't fear! God will be with you wherever you go. God protects you!**

Leader Tip

You could also use this game when you're teaching about Noah and the ark. How did Noah have courage? How did God protect Noah and his family?

Be Strong!

Topic: Courage

Scripture: Joshua 1:7a

Game Overview: Kids will run a relay race in two different ways.

✩ ✩ ✩ ✩ ✩

Supplies: Bible, stopwatch

Preparation: None needed

Have kids form two or three equal teams and get on their knees along one side of the room. Say: **When I ask, "You got a problem?" the first person in each team will crawl to the opposite wall on hands and knees. When you get to the wall, touch it and shout, "Be strong and courageous!" Then stand up, run back, and tag the next person in your team who will then crawl to the wall! Ready? You got a problem?**

✩ ✩ ✩ ✩ ✩

Time the teams, and then race again and encourage teams to beat their times. At the end of the game, gather kids and read Joshua 1:7. Discuss the following questions:

• **What was it like to crawl during the first part of this relay? to run during the second part?**

• **How are problems in life like the first part of the relay?**

• **How does God give you courage to face problems?**

Say: **No matter what happens in life, God tells us to be strong and courageous. God gives us courage because God is always with us.**

Leader Tip

This game is best played on carpet, *not* tile. If necessary, adapt the first leg of the relay in any way that limits mobility, such as having kids crab walk or skip backward.

Daniel Escapes

Topic: Courage

Scripture: Daniel 10:12

Game Overview: Kids will have courage as they escape from a circle.

☆ ☆ ☆ ☆ ☆

Supplies: Bible

Preparation: Clear the center of your classroom of all furniture and equipment, or play this game outdoors.

Gather kids in a circle, and have them hold hands and stand very close together. Choose one child to be in the middle of the circle.

Say: **When I say "Go," the person in the middle will try to escape the circle by crawling between the legs of two people. If that person is successful, the kids on both sides of the escape hole will join the person and they'll all go to the center of the circle. I'll say "Go" again, and all three of you will try to escape. Ready? Go!**

Play the game, and keep repeating it until too few kids are left to form the outer circle.

☆ ☆ ☆ ☆ ☆

At the end of the game, gather kids and read aloud Daniel 10:12. Then discuss the following questions:

• **When did you have to have courage in this game?**

• **When do you need courage each day?**

• **Who helps you have courage?**

Say: **In the church, it's important that we help one another have courage and stand strong in our faith. God gives all of us strength to help one another. God is with us always!**

Broken Bubbles

Topic: David

Scripture: 1 Samuel 20:42; 2 Samuel 9:1-7

Game Overview: Kids will participate in a bubble relay and learn how David and Jonathan kept promises.

☆ ☆ ☆ ☆ ☆

Supplies: Bible, bottle of bubble solution, bubble wand
Preparation: None needed

Have kids form two groups, and ask them to line up at opposite sides of the room, facing each other. Give the first person in one group a container of bubble solution and a bubble wand.

Say: [Name of person] **will blow a bubble. Then** [he or she] **will blow the bubble across the room to the first person in the next line, give that person the bubble solution, then stay on that side. The new person will blow the** *same* **bubble, if it still exists, back to the next person standing in line on the opposite side. Continue until everyone has blown the bubble and traded sides. If the bubble pops, simply blow a new one and keep going. Ready? Go!**

Play until everyone has had a turn to blow a bubble across the room. Then collect the bubble solution and wand.

☆ ☆ ☆ ☆ ☆

After the game, discuss the following questions:
• **What did you notice about the bubbles?**
• **What helped you successfully move the bubbles?**
• **In what ways do these bubbles remind you of promises?**

Say: **It was hard to control the breakable bubbles, and it can be hard to follow through when we make promises. But God wants us to be faithful friends who keep our promises. Let's learn about a promise that David made to his best friend, Jonathan.**

Read aloud 1 Samuel 20:42 and 2 Samuel 9:1-7. Then ask:
• **How did David keep his promise?**
• **Why did David keep his promise to Jonathan?**

Say: **It can be hard to keep some promises. Sometimes, it seems like it would be easier to just let the promise break, kind of like our bubbles. But real friends keep their promises.**

Goliath Can't Catch Me

Topic: David

Scripture: 1 Samuel 17

Game Overview: Kids will try to escape Goliath in this game.

☆ ☆ ☆ ☆ ☆

Supplies: Bible

Preparation: None needed

Choose one person to be Goliath. Have that person stand in the middle of the room. Explain that Goliath can't move his or her feet, but can bend over to tag children.

Other players must see how close they can get to Goliath without getting tagged. Each child who gets tagged should join Goliath and, without moving his or her feet, try to tag others.

☆ ☆ ☆ ☆ ☆

Continue playing until everyone's been tagged. Then have kids sit close together and hook arms while you tell them the story about young David beating the giant Goliath. Say: **Goliath was huge, and lots of people were afraid of him. Goliath had beaten lots of people in his time, kind of like he tagged all of us.** Ask:

• **How would you feel if you came face to face with the giant Goliath?**

Say: **I think I might be afraid, but a young boy named David had no fear of the giant. He said, "I come against you in the name of the Lord Almighty!"** Have kids repeat the phrase. **Then David picked up a stone, threw it, and it hit the giant.** Have kids scatter from their close circle to any place around the room. **God helped David beat the giant.**

Have kids play the game again, and then take turns retelling the story of how David beat Goliath.

Human Slingshots

Topic: David

Scripture: 1 Samuel 17

Game Overview: With partners, kids will make human sling-shots and try to hit a target.

☆ ☆ ☆ ☆ ☆

Supplies: Bible, newspapers, red construction paper, tape, rubber band

Preparation: Make a target by taping to a wall two long strips of red construction paper in an X. Set a stack of newspapers about ten feet from the target.

Ask kids to sit by the stack of newspaper. Briefly tell them the story of how young David beat the giant Goliath (1 Samuel 17). Say: **Let's have a little target practice. We'll use paper stones and human slingshots!**

Help kids find partners, and then have them stand anywhere around the room. To form a "sling," each pair must stand side by side and interlace the fingers of their closest hands. Before making a stone from paper, each pair should practice moving their connected arms as one. Help kids get an idea of how they should attempt to move their arms. Hold up a rubber band or a regular sling-shot and show kids how to pull back and release the band.

Each pair should then use its paper stone to load its human slingshot. Then pairs should take aim at the target. Each time a pair hits the target, partners take one step back.

☆ ☆ ☆ ☆ ☆

At the end of the game, have kids collect all the paper stones from the playing area, and congratulate each of your "slingers"! Discuss the following questions:

• **What was it like for you and your partner to try to hit the target?**

• **What do you think it was like for David to try to hit Goliath?**

Say: **God was with David that day. Through God's power and David's faith, God helped young David beat the big giant Goliath.**

Sittin' and Tuggin'

Topic: Difficulties

Scripture: Ecclesiastes 4:9-12

Game Overview: Kids will play Tug of War in various ways.

☆ ☆ ☆ ☆ ☆

Supplies: Bible, masking tape, twenty-foot length of rope, handkerchief

Preparation: Tie the handkerchief at the ten-foot mark of the rope. If you don't have a rope, securely tie together several jump ropes. Place two pieces of masking tape on the floor, three feet apart. Lay the rope across the masking tape so that the handkerchief is in the middle of the two pieces of tape.

Form two teams of children, and have them take their positions on either side of the rope. Say: **Let's play Tug of War in a lot of different ways. Don't worry about winning or losing in this game, because we'll switch teams lots of times and we'll switch ways of tugging lots of times. We'll all help one another in this game of difficult daring!**

Have kids sit on the ground. Have each child hold one hand on the rope and the other hand on his or her head. At your signal, children will pull—with only one hand. When a team has pulled the handkerchief on the rope past a piece of tape, have everyone clap.

Randomly and frequently, have team members switch places. Add variety by adding rounds in which children may pull with just their thumbs and forefingers, their toes, or their pinkies.

☆ ☆ ☆ ☆ ☆

At the end of each round, have all kids clap for one another. Then form a circle with the rope, and have kids hold onto it for a discussion time. Discuss the following questions:

- **What was difficult in this game?**
- **How did your friends help you?**

Read Ecclesiastes 4:9-12; then ask:

- **According to this verse, who helps us?**
- **How does God help you in difficult times?**

Say: **God cares when we have problems or difficulties in life. God surrounds us with family and friends and the church to help us.**

Oddball Bowling

Topic: Difficulties

Scripture: Deuteronomy 31:6

Game Overview: Kids will play a wacky game of bowling.

☆ ☆ ☆ ☆ ☆

Supplies: Bible, volleyball, small bag of sunflower seeds or candies, nine empty two-liter plastic bottles, duct tape

Preparation: Use duct tape to secure a small bag of sunflower seeds or small candies to the side of a volleyball. Completely cover the bag with tape so it doesn't break during the game.

Ask kids to tell you some difficult times they or some friends might be facing. For each thing they say, set up a two-liter bottle in the middle of your room. Instead of a bowling game formation, set the bottles in a square shape.

Form two teams, and have teams stand at opposite sides of your room, with the bowling pins in the middle.

Say: **I have a difficult situation for your teams to work on, and then you'll get a treat. The difficult situation is for you to work together to knock down a total of ninety-nine pins. When you've worked it out, you'll get a treat!**

Give the volleyball to the first person in line at one end of the room, and have that person roll the ball and knock down as many pins as possible. Have the first person in line at the other end of the room retrieve the ball and roll it back at the pins. Keep alternating turns until all the pins are down. Then reset the pins, and have kids go at it again. Encourage kids to cheer for one another, because every pin knocked down gets them one step closer to their treat.

Leader Tip

The purpose of the bag taped to the ball is to make it off-balance so it rolls erratically—thus causing another difficulty for kids to work through!

☆ ☆ ☆ ☆ ☆

Call time after kids have knocked down ninety-nine pins. Then serve the seeds or candies that were taped to the volleyball. Discuss the following questions:

- **What was difficult in this game?**
- **How did you work together to finally get the treat?**
- **What difficulties do you face at school? home?**

Read Deuteronomy 31:6, and ask:

• Who helps you with those tough times?

Say: **Whenever we face a tough time, we can always turn to God. He will help us; he never leaves us.**

Cotton Nose Blowers

Topic: Difficulties

Scripture: Hebrews 12:1-2

Game Overview: Kids will use their noses to carry cotton balls across a line.

☆ ☆ ☆ ☆ ☆

Supplies: Bible, cotton balls, petroleum jelly, masking tape, baby wipes

Preparation: Clear a playing area, and set out the supplies. Make a masking tape line about five feet from a wall. Spread the cotton balls along the wall.

Give each child a chance to carry cotton balls across a line and drop them. Kids will try to carry as many cotton balls as they can within a one-minute time limit. Sound easy? Not too difficult? Well, there's a catch. Kids may carry the cotton balls only on their noses.

Help each child smear some petroleum jelly on his or her nose. Then ask kids to get on their hands and knees and poke their noses onto cotton balls on the floor. When a child gets a cotton ball to stick, the child will crawl to the line and disengage the cotton by blowing. Kids may use their hands for nothing but crawling.

☆ ☆ ☆ ☆ ☆

At the end of the game, count the cotton balls and wipe off noses. Then discuss the following questions:

• **What was easy about this game? difficult?**

• **What's the best tip you have to give someone to successfully do this game?**

Read Hebrews 12:1-2, and ask:

• **According to this verse, who helps us through difficult times?**

Say: **We're surrounded by people who love us. We can laugh together even when we go through life's ups and downs. No matter what difficulties we face, we know heaven waits for all who believe.**

Unseen Presence

Topic: Faith

Scripture: Hebrews 11:1

Game Overview: Kids will search through uncooked rice for "hidden" things.

☆ ☆ ☆ ☆ ☆

Supplies: Bible, blindfolds, bowls full of uncooked rice, paper clips

Preparation: For each group of four, you'll need a blindfold and a bowl filled with rice mixed with about twenty-five paper clips. Set out the supplies in the playing area.

Have kids form groups of four, and give each group its blindfold and bowl. Say: **In your group, choose one person to be your "seeker." Blindfold your seeker.** Pause and help kids to do this. **Now, seekers, you have one minute to find as many paper clips as you can in the bowl of rice. Ready? Go!**

Call time after one minute. Then have kids count the "found" clips. Let kids remix the paper clips in the rice and choose another seeker.

☆ ☆ ☆ ☆ ☆

After everyone has had a chance to be the seeker, gather everyone in a circle. Discuss the following questions:

• **How many paper clips did you find?**

• **How easy or difficult was it to find the paper clips in the rice? What made it easy? What made it difficult?**

Read Hebrews 11:1; then say: **Just as we hunted for something we couldn't see or feel, God asks us to believe in things we can't see or feel.** Ask:

• **How can you be sure that you're believing in something real if you can't see or feel it?**

Say: **The paper clips were here all the time, and God is here all the time too. We can believe in God even though we don't always see or feel what we're believing in.**

The River Bend

Topic: Faith

Scripture: Proverbs 3:5-6

Game Overview: Kids will lean on each other and help each other cross a river.

☆ ☆ ☆ ☆ ☆

Supplies: Bible, masking tape, pillows

Preparation: Use masking tape to make a large V on the ground. This will represent a river. The "river" should be very narrow at one end and gradually widen until it's more than seven feet across. Place several pillows within the wide end of the river.

Help children form pairs. This game will work best if partners are about the same size. Gather children near the narrow end of the river.

Say: **Look at this river! You can't see them, but below the surface of this river, alligators and snakes lurk. Since we don't want to fall into the river, we're going to have to make bridges with our partners. We're going to trust and have faith that our partners will help us.**

Ask one pair to stand at the narrowest point of the river. Tell these partners to face each other and clasp hands. Then have the partners walk along their respective banks of the river (the sides of the V). As the river widens, the children will have to move farther apart. As they move farther along the river, have them lean in and bear each other's weight. See how far they can progress before one or

both of them fall into the river. The pillows will soften their fall!

Repeat this with all the other pairs. After one pair has moved a few feet down the river, another pair may start so the game will move along at a quicker pace. If children would like to improve their distances, let them try again.

★ ★ ★ ★ ★

After everyone has had at least one turn, gather children and discuss the following questions:

• **What was your strategy in this activity?**
• **Why was it important to have faith in your partner?**
• **In what ways do we have faith and "lean on" God?**

Read Proverbs 3:5-6; then say: **This game shows how important faith is! And having faith in God is even more important than trusting a partner, because God is the only one who can save us.**

Dinosaur Egg Hunt

Topic: Family

Scripture: Luke 11:9-13

Game Overview: Kids will work in "families" and go on a unique egg hunt.

☆ ☆ ☆ ☆ ☆

Supplies: Bible, large bowl, knife, small bowls, forks, various kinds of fruit that might pass for dinosaur eggs (watermelons, cantaloupes, grapefruits, oranges)

Preparation: Choose whether to play the game inside or outside. Then hide the dinosaur eggs inside among the pillows and cushions of couches and chairs, behind chairs, or on bookshelves. Or hide the eggs outside among leaves, weeds, tall grasses, or pine needles.

When kids arrive, form "family groups" of four to five kids. Say: **God gave us families to care for us each day. No families look the same! Some families have one mom or dad, and some have grandparents or guardians. But no matter what families look like, God wants all family members to work together, help and encourage one another, and be kind to one another. Let's play a game and pretend we're members of a family who are helping one another.**

Explain that dinosaurs have been seen in the area, and kids have been asked to look for the eggs. Encourage kids to work with their families, being kind to one another, walking together, talking together, and helping carry the eggs to one spot in your classroom. Tell the families that it's very important to find the eggs before they hatch, or there'll be a dinosaur population explosion. Describe the eggs' colors, sizes, and shapes.

Send families out to look for the eggs, and have them bring the eggs back to a central location. After someone has found one egg, the idea will catch on. After all of the eggs have been found, have the group make a dinosaur egg salad.

☆ ☆ ☆ ☆ ☆

As kids eat the dinosaur egg salad, discuss the following questions:

• **What was it like to work together with your family groups?**

• **How is this like or unlike your family at home?**

Read Luke 11:9-13, and ask:

• **What does this verse tell us about families?**

Say: **God gives us people to love us on earth, but God is our Father in heaven. God loves us so much and cares for us forever.**

Little Squirt

Topic: Family

Scripture: Ephesians 3:14-15

Game Overview: Kids will race to squirt designs on paper towels as they talk about their families.

☆ ☆ ☆ ☆ ☆

Supplies: Bible, white paper towels, three squirt guns, three buckets of water, tape, food coloring (blue, red, and yellow)

Preparation: This game works best outside. Warn kids ahead of time to wear old clothes. Fill three buckets with water, and add one color of food coloring to each. Fill three squirt guns before the game. Tape several white paper towels to a tree or old chair. Set the buckets five feet away from the paper towels.

Have kids form three groups, and have each group line up behind a bucket. Give someone in each group a squirt gun. Say: **Let's learn something about your families as you play this game. The first question is, "How old is the youngest person in your family?" When I say "Go," run to the paper towels and squirt them once for every year. For example, if you have a three-year-old brother, you'll squirt the paper towels three times. Then run back, and give the squirt gun to the next person in your line. Ready? Go!**

Continue by having kids squirt their answers to these questions:

• **How many people are in your family?**

• **How many pets are in your family?**

• **How many cans of pop does your parent or guardian allow you to drink in a day?**

Every now and then, call time so you can untape the paper towels and lay them in the sun to dry. Provide fresh paper towels, and have kids continue squirting until everyone's had at least one turn. Continue asking questions like those above so kids learn more about one another and their families.

☆ ☆ ☆ ☆ ☆

At the end of the game, discuss the following questions:

• **What did you learn about one another and your families?**

• **How are you alike? different?**

Read Ephesians 3:14-15; then ask:

• **What does this verse tell us we are?**

Say: **We live with all kinds of families, and we also are the family of God!**

When the "decorated" paper towels are dry, let kids help you tape them together to form a quilt. Hang the quilt in your church or classroom as a reminder of each special member in the family of God!

Heart Wash

Topic: Forgiveness

Scripture: Acts 22:16

Game Overview: Kids will wash blobs from balloons in a race.

☆ ☆ ☆ ☆ ☆

Supplies: Bible, ten red balloons, table, masking tape, one or two cans of hair-styling mousse, two spray bottles, stopwatch or watch with second hand, towels

Preparation: This game works best if you play it outside. However, if you play it inside, cover the area with a tarp. Inflate ten red balloons. Securely tape five of the balloons in a row to the edge of a table. Set the extra balloons aside to use as replacements in case the original balloons break. Use masking tape to mark a line on the ground about five feet from the table. Fill both spray bottles.

> ### Leader Tip
>
> Spray bottles should have adjustable nozzles so they can send long, straight streams of water. Misters won't work for this game.

Have kids form two teams and line up behind the masking tape line. Use the mousse to cover the front of each balloon. As you do this, say: **Let's pretend these balloons are our hearts and these blobs are the bad**

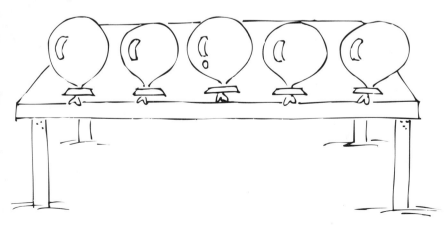

feelings that cover our hearts when we don't love and forgive others.

Give the first person in each team a spray bottle. Explain that they'll have fifteen seconds to spray as many of the blobs from the balloons as possible. When you call time, the first "sprayers" will hand the bottles to the next kids in line, and so on.

✯ ✯ ✯ ✯ ✯

When each child has had a turn to spray, count the number of balloon "hearts" that have been washed clean. Then discuss the following questions:

· **What got the blobs off the balloons?**
· **Who cleans the blobs of sin from our hearts?**

Read Acts 22:16; then say: **When we tell Jesus we're sorry, he forgives us. Jesus washes away our sin and makes our hearts clean again.**

Try, Try Again

Topic: Forgiveness

Scripture: Ephesians 2:8-9

Game Overview: Kids will attempt a task that isn't as easy as anticipated.

☆ ☆ ☆ ☆ ☆

Supplies: Bible, masking tape

Preparation: Place a ten-foot strip of masking tape on the center of the floor.

Have kids stand in a circle around the tape line. Say: **I wonder if it's possible to walk along this line without stepping off. It looks pretty difficult. Do you think you could do it?** Ask for a volunteer to attempt to walk the line. As the volunteer comes forward, say: **One thing I forgot to tell you—before you try to make it across, you need to turn around like this.**

Carefully spin the first volunteer about ten times, and have him or her start at one end of the line and walk across to the other end. Let each child have a chance to spin around and then try to balance all the way across the line.

☆ ☆ ☆ ☆ ☆

When everyone has had a turn to walk the line, have kids sit in a circle. Discuss the following questions:

• **What did you think when I first asked if you could walk on the line?**

• **How did your thoughts change?**

Say: **Sometimes we think we can "do" things to earn God's forgiveness. But the more we try, the more we fail.**

Read Ephesians 2:8-9. Say: **Our sins are forgiven only because of Jesus, not because of anything we can do.** Have kids again walk the line, but this time don't spin them. Hold each child's hand as he or she walks across the line and have the child say, "Thanks for Jesus."

Chair Snatchers

Topic: Friendship

Scripture: 3 John 14

Game Overview: Kids will get to know one another while they snatch chairs.

★ ★ ★ ★ ★

Supplies: Bible, chairs

Preparation: Place chairs in a close circle. Have enough chairs for everyone minus one.

Choose one child to be the "chair snatcher" and to stand in the center of the circle. Have the rest of the group sit in the chairs.

When the chair snatcher yells "Rumble," begin the game. Players will move one chair to the right while the chair snatcher tries to find a seat to sit in. Movement continues to the right until the chair snatcher says "Reverse." Then everyone will move to the left. The chair snatcher may call "Reverse" at any time. When the chair snatcher finally snatches a seat, the person to his or her left becomes the new chair snatcher.

After the first successful snatch, ask the new chair snatcher to say his or her name and say what the snatcher likes to play with friends. Then go around the circle and have everyone quickly share.

Continue to play. Each time you get a new chair snatcher, ask another get-to-know-you question, such as "What's your favorite vegetable?" "What's the best cartoon you've ever seen?" or "Who's your favorite movie actor?" After the chair snatcher has answered, go around the circle and listen to everyone else's answers.

☆ ☆ ☆ ☆ ☆

At the end of the game, pull in another chair and have the last chair snatcher sit in it. Then discuss the following questions:

- **What did you like about this game?**
- **What did you learn about your friends today?**

Say: **Good friends get to know one another and have fun together.**

Read 3 John 14. Then have kids go around the circle and each say to the person on the right, "Hi, [name of friend], glad you're here today." Say: **Sometimes we might feel left out, as we did when we were chair snatchers. Good friends welcome one another and greet one another by name.**

Potato Pass

Topic: Friendship

Scripture: Proverbs 17:17a

Game Overview: Kids will work with friends as they pass potatoes with their feet.

☆ ☆ ☆ ☆ ☆

Supplies: Bible, potatoes, rope or yarn

Preparation: Place a length of rope or yarn on the floor to form a squiggly path around the room.

Have kids form pairs, and give each pair a potato. Have all pairs line up at the beginning of the path. Say: **We're going to work with our partners to move the potatoes along the path. You can't use your hands to move your potato! Use your feet to move the potato as you would a soccer ball. You can touch the potato with your feet only three times, and then you have to pass it to your partner. Keep passing back and forth as you work together to get your potato to the end of the path. Say encouraging words and be helpful!**

One at a time, have pairs start along the path. As pairs complete their journey, have them sit down and clap for the others as they finish. When everyone has finished, have kids form a giant huddle and pat one another's backs.

☆ ☆ ☆ ☆ ☆

At the end of the game, discuss the following questions:

• **How did you help each other follow the path? What encouraging words did you use?**

• **How is this like friends helping each other each day?**

Read Proverbs 17:17a, then ask:

• **What does this verse tell us about friends?**

• **Besides helping one another and saying encouraging words, how do we show love to our friends?**

Say: **A friend loves at all times. We show love to friends when we help them, say encouraging words, are kind to them, include them in games, and have fun together. Jesus is our best friend! Jesus loves us, helps us, and encourages us always.**

Name That Vocalist

Topic: Gifts

Scripture: 1 Corinthians 12:4-6

Game Overview: Kids will wear blindfolds and try to recognize someone singing in their ears.

☆ ☆ ☆ ☆ ☆

Supplies: Bible, chairs, blindfolds

Preparation: Arrange chairs in a big circle, and place a blindfold on every other chair.

Ask each of the kids to sit on a chair. If a child sits on a chair that has a blindfold, have the child put it on. Encourage kids without blindfolds to help tie the blindfolds on the others. Have the sighted kids mix and find new chairs so the blindfolded children don't know who's sitting next to them.

Say: **When I shout "Sing!" those of you without blindfolds should each sing your favorite song into the ear of the person on your left. You don't necessarily need to sing the same song. You could sing "Jesus Loves Me" or "Deep and Wide" or "My God Is So Great" or your choice! If you're wearing a blindfold, listen to the person singing in your ear and try to guess who it is. Ready? Sing!**

When everyone has guessed, have kids take off the blindfolds to see who really was sharing such a lovely gift in their ears! Then switch roles and continue to share everyone's gift of singing.

☆ ☆ ☆ ☆ ☆

At the end of the game, gather the blindfolds, and discuss the following questions:

• **Besides singing, what other gifts did you use during this game?**

Say: **You not only sang, you heard a song, recognized a voice, saw a friend, and shared a good laugh together. You all are gifts in this room!**

Read 1 Corinthians 12:4-6; then ask:

• **What do these verses tell us about gifts?**

• **What other gifts has God blessed you with?**

• **How can you use your gifts to share Jesus' love with others?**

Close by sharing your gifts together. Sing one more praise song in unison!

Gift Bow Giveaway

Topic: Gifts

Scripture: Malachi 3:10

Game Overview: Kids will give away bows, not expecting any gifts in return.

☆ ☆ ☆ ☆ ☆

Supplies: Bible, gift bows, bag of snacks

Preparation: Place a gift bow on the snack bag.

Give each person six gift bows. Ask participants to stick the bows to their clothing. Say: **When I say, "Give a gift," try to give away your bows by attaching them to other people's clothing. The goal is to give away all your bows without receiving any from other players. Ready? Give a gift!**

☆ ☆ ☆ ☆ ☆

Stop the trading after several minutes, and gather the kids in a circle. Discuss the following questions:

• **What was it like for you to give away your gift bows in this game?**
• **What kind of gifts do you give in real life?**

Read Malachi 3:10; then ask:

• **What does this say about giving gifts to God?**
• **What can you give to God to show him how much you love him?**

Bring out the bag of snacks with a gift bow on it. Pass the bag around and ask each child to get a snack, give it to someone sitting by him or her, then eat and enjoy. Say: **You are gifts to me! Our good God has blessed us with so many gifts! Let's always be generous and give to others.**

Surrounded by Love

Topic: God's love

Scripture: Psalm 32:10

Game Overview: Kids will pass a hula hoop around a circle without letting go of one another's hands.

☆ ☆ ☆ ☆ ☆

Supplies: Bible, two hula hoops

Preparation: None needed

Leader Tip

This game works best if you have no more than ten or fifteen kids in a circle. No hula hoop? Substitute several clean pieces of pantyhose tied together.

Ask kids to form a large circle with the hula hoop resting on a child's arm.

Say: **The goal of this game is to work the hula hoop around the circle without letting go of one another's hands. You'll need to figure out how to get it over your head, climb through it, and pass it on— without breaking the circle. Ready? Go!**

Play again, but this time pass another hula hoop in the opposite direction, so you have two hula hoops going around the circle.

☆ ☆ ☆ ☆ ☆

At the end of the game, discuss this question:

• **How did you pass the hula hoop around the circle?**

Say: **At times in this game, you were surrounded by the hula hoop. It covered you from your head to your toes!**

Read Psalm 32:10; then ask:

• **What does this verse say about God's love?**

• **How have you seen God's love in your life? in someone else's life?**

Say: **Just as we experienced with our hula hoops, God surrounds us with his love. God's love covers us from our head to our toes!**

It's Spreading!

Topic: God's love

Scripture: Acts 2

Game Overview: Kids will make a long chain of God's love that reaches around the room.

☆ ☆ ☆ ☆ ☆

Supplies: Bible

Preparation: None needed

Say: **Let's play a game that will show us how God's love spreads. Let's try to wrap God's love around the room.**

Ask everyone to stand against the wall in a line. Have the first child lie on the floor with his or her hands on the starting line and feet stretched in the direction kids will wrap around the room. As soon as the first child lies down, the second child will run and grab the feet of the first child and also lie down. As soon as the second child lies down, the third child will grab the second child's feet and lie down, and so on. As kids run, have them say "[Child's name], God loves you" to the people whose feet they grab. Keep going until kids have wrapped the room in God's love.

☆ ☆ ☆ ☆ ☆

At the end of the game, ask the following questions:

• **What did you like about spreading around the room in this game?**

• **How is that like God's love?**

Summarize the story of Pentecost in Acts 2; then say: **When we tell people about God's love, it grows! Peter talked to a crowd about God's love. Verse 41 says that *3,000 people* came to believe in God that day! Wow! When we tell others, God's love spreads! God's love spreads around the room, the church, our homes, our neighborhoods, and the whole world!**

Big and Bigger Tag

Topic: God's love

Scripture: Ephesians 3:17b-19

Game Overview: Kids will be tagged by a sheet and add on to it so it grows.

☆ ☆ ☆ ☆ ☆

Supplies: Bible, bedsheet

Preparation: Clear a large area indoors, or mark boundaries and play outside.

Gather kids in a circle, and ask a volunteer to be "It." Give the volunteer a bedsheet to hold.

Say: **In this game, the person holding the sheet will try to tag you by touching you with the sheet or wrapping it around you. If you get tagged, you'll then join the person by grabbing one end of the sheet and both of you will try to catch another. Each time you catch someone, the person will join you in holding onto the sheet. Hold the sheet at waist level, no higher! Let's see how big we can make the sheet!**

☆ ☆ ☆ ☆ ☆

At the end of the game, discuss the following questions:

· **What did you like about this game?**

Leader Tip

If your group is larger than ten kids, use two bedsheets and have two volunteers be "It" for the first round. Kids can eventually join hands to link both bedsheets so they form a chain. Remind kids throughout the game to hold the sheets at waist level, no higher. That way, kids won't inadvertently get knocked down by the sheets.

- What happened to the sheet as more kids held it?
- How is this like God's love spreading and growing?

Read Ephesians 3:17b-19; then ask:

- What does this verse tell us about God's love?

Say: **God's love is wide, long, high, and deep! When God's love touches us, we just want to share it with others. God's love grows and spreads. Let's tell others how much God loves them!**

A Christmas Gift

Topic: Jesus' birth

Scripture: Matthew 2:1-12; Luke 1:26-38; 2:1-20

Game Overview: Kids will experience the joy of giving while they listen to the Christmas story.

☆ ☆ ☆ ☆ ☆

Supplies: Bible

Preparation: Ask kids to bring a wrapped gift to give to either a boy or girl. Set the cost of the gift low so all can participate. Bring a few extra gifts in case kids forget to bring one.

Ask kids to hold their gifts and sit in a circle. Say: **I'll read the Christmas story. As I read, pass your gift to the person on your right every time I read the words "God," "Lord," and "Jesus." When I've finished, I'll say "Amen," and you'll keep the gift that's in your hands at that time.**

☆ ☆ ☆ ☆ ☆

Read aloud Matthew 2:1-12; Luke 1:26-38; and Luke 2:1-20. When you've finished, say "Amen." Have kids hold their gifts as you ask the following questions:

- What did you have to do to receive the gift you have?
- What did we have to do to receive the gift of Jesus?
- How many things can you remember about the Bible story?

Say: **Jesus is the greatest gift of all! He freely gave his life. Because of Jesus, we'll live forever with him and everyone else who loves him, too.**

Celebrate the gift of Jesus by letting the kids open and enjoy their gifts!

Bethlehem Balloons

Topic: Jesus' birth

Scripture: Luke 2:1-20

Game Overview: Kids will take a census of balloons.

✮ ✮ ✮ ✮ ✮

Supplies: Bible, balloons (one balloon per child, an equal number of balloons in four colors)

Preparation: Have kids help you inflate and tie balloons before the game (older children can help the younger ones), or ask a volunteer to help you. Place the balloons in the center of your room.

Give each child a balloon. Ask kids to scatter around the room so they're equally spaced throughout your playing area, and have them sit down.

Say: **It's time to take a census of the balloons. A census is when leaders count how many people actually live in their city or area.** Read aloud Luke 2:1-5. **In fact, Joseph had to take Mary to his hometown to be counted in a census. Joseph's hometown was Bethlehem. Well, all our balloons must be counted, and to be counted they must return to their "hometowns."**

The hometowns are the corners of your playing area. Assign one color to each corner to designate which corners are the homes of which color balloons.

Say: **There's one catch with the balloon census: The balloons must be batted to the correct corners, and you can't stand up or move from your spots.**

Tell kids when to begin, and then stand back and watch the fun! When all the balloons have been batted to the corners, close the game by asking each child to go to a corner, find one balloon, and sit on it to break it. As each child breaks a balloon, help him or her count out "one" and so on until kids have counted all the balloons in each corner.

✮ ✮ ✮ ✮ ✮

At the end of the game, discuss the following questions:

• **How easy or hard was it for you to get your balloon to its corner?**

• **How is that like how Joseph and Mary might have felt when they had to go to Bethlehem to be counted in a census?**

• **What do you think their trip was like?**

Read the rest of the story from Luke 2:6-20.

Bethlehem Builders

Topic: Jesus' birth

Scripture: Matthew 2:1-12; Luke 1:26-38; 2:1-20

Game Overview: Kids will build Bethlehem and tell the story of Jesus' birth.

☆ ☆ ☆ ☆ ☆

Supplies: Bible, building blocks and boxes of various sizes

Preparation: Put all the building supplies in the center of your room.

Invite kids to form small groups of four to five. Give each group an equal number of building blocks and boxes. Encourage kids to think about the Christmas story and what it must have been like in Bethlehem. Have kids take a few minutes to build things that were in Bethlehem the night Jesus was born, such as a stable, manger, inn, animals, or trees. Tell them they also can use anything else in the room as building supplies, such as chairs, tables, or books. While they build, read aloud the story of Jesus' birth: Matthew 2:1-12; Luke 1:26-38; and Luke 2:1-20.

When everyone has finished building, gather kids together and have them take turns telling the story of the first Christmas, using what they've made.

☆ ☆ ☆ ☆ ☆

At the end of the game, discuss the following questions:

• **What do you think it was like when Jesus was born?**

• **How can you give thanks to Jesus for coming to save us?**

Sing some Christmas songs and carols to celebrate and praise Jesus for coming to save us from our sins.

Shin Tag

Topic: Jesus' miracles
Scripture: Mark 2:1-12
Game Overview: Kids will grab their shins and try to run.

☆ ☆ ☆ ☆ ☆

Supplies: Bible
Preparation: None needed

Show kids where their shins are—the area between the knees and ankles. Tell children that on "Go," they'll run around the room and try to tag others by touching their shins. When a child's shin gets tagged, that child must hold onto the shin with one hand and run in this position. If kids get tagged on both shins, they have to sit down and try to tag others if the others get too close. If kids succeed in tagging someone who runs by them, they can get up and run again.

☆ ☆ ☆ ☆ ☆

At the end of the game, discuss the following questions:
• **What was easy about playing this game? hard?**
• **What do you think it would be like if you couldn't walk?**

Ask whether kids have had any broken bones or know anyone who can't walk. Read the story of Jesus healing the lame man (Mark 2:1-12). Then ask:
• **How do you think the man felt before he met Jesus?**
• **How do you think the man felt after Jesus healed him?**

Let kids play the game again and think about how the lame man must have felt happy and grateful that he could walk again.

Elastic circle

Topic: Jesus' miracles

Scripture: Mark 6:30-42

Game Overview: Kids will pretend to be an elastic band and will stretch as they hear the story of Jesus feeding the 5,000.

☆ ☆ ☆ ☆ ☆

Supplies: Bible, masking tape

Preparation: None needed

Ask kids to stand and hold hands in a circle. Say: **Let's play a game in which you'll pretend you're an elastic band. First, start out very small.** Have kids bunch together, so they're shoulder to shoulder, yet still in a circle shape. **Now, stretch out as far as possible.** Pause while kids do this. Use strips of masking tape to mark off how far the group stretches. Ask kids to go back into the small circle and again stand shoulder to shoulder. **Now, let's see if we can get our elastic band to stretch even farther! The catch is, you have to touch someone at all times.** Brainstorm ways kids might make the circle stretch even farther. For example, kids could touch fingertips, or they could lay down and touch fingers to a neighbor's toes. Continue finding ways to stretch the elastic band. Move the masking tape to mark each stretch.

☆ ☆ ☆ ☆ ☆

After several rounds, ask kids to come back together and sit down in a circle. Discuss these questions:

- **How did we get our small circle to stretch bigger each time?**
- **What else do you know that starts out small, then gets big?**

Read aloud Mark 6:30-42, and tell the story of how Jesus took a little bit of food and made it grow so that it fed 5,000 people! They even had leftovers.

Let kids review the story in a fun way. Ask them to form pairs and pretend to be tiny elastic bands. Have pairs hold hands, go in, then stretch out far, then go back in and tell one thing they remember about the story.

Next, have kids form trios and do the same thing, then tell something else they remember about the story.

Continue in this manner until kids again have formed one giant elastic band. Give a prayer of thanks that Jesus could take a little food and make it grow to feed so many people!

Butterfly Breakout

Topic: Jesus' resurrection

Scripture: John 20:1-23

Game Overview: Kids will race with a balloon butterfly.

☆ ☆ ☆ ☆ ☆

Supplies: Bible, 2-60 balloons (the long, skinny balloons used to create balloon animals), balloon pump or bicycle pump, masking tape or rope, watch with a second hand, whistle

Preparation: Use a pump to inflate the balloons. Fill the balloons, but don't over-inflate them. Tie together the two ends of a 2-60 balloon to create a circle. Hold the knot in one hand and the opposite end of the balloon in the other hand. Bring these together, and twist to create a figure eight. This creates a simple butterfly. Make one butterfly for every group of five to six children. Use the masking tape or rope to mark a starting line.

Form teams of five to six kids, and have them line up behind the starting line. Tell kids that these lines are their cocoons. Give a balloon butterfly to the last person in each line. When you give a signal, that person will pass the butterfly over his or her head to the next person. As soon as the child has passed the butterfly, he or she will run to the front of the line. This way, the butterfly will continually move overhead toward the front of the line, just as if it's flying. If a butterfly touches the ground, everyone in the team has to freeze, count to ten, pick up the butterfly, and get it flying again!

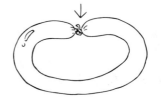

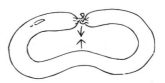

Give a signal to begin, and then blow your whistle after one minute. See which team has gotten its butterfly farthest from the cocoon. If time permits,

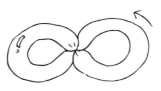

play the game again to see whether teams can improve their technique and speed.

☆ ☆ ☆ ☆ ☆

Then collect the butterfly balloons, gather everyone, and ask:

• **How can a butterfly remind us of Jesus?**

Say: **Just as a cocoon can't hold a butterfly after it's out, the grave couldn't hold Jesus any longer. Jesus has risen from the dead and will never die again. When we know Jesus, we have new life too.**

Gone Fishing

Topic: Jesus' resurrection

Scripture: John 21:1-14

Game Overview: Kids will go fishing for ice.

☆ ☆ ☆ ☆ ☆

Supplies: Bible, wading pool filled with water, two bags of ice cubes, plastic cups (one for every child), towels

Preparation: If you play inside, lay a tarp on the floor and then set up the pool. Empty two bags of ice cubes into the pool.

Ask kids to remove their shoes and socks, then gather around the pool. Read aloud John 21:1-3; then say: **When Jesus died and was buried, several of his disciples got on a boat and went fishing. They must have been sad as they sat on that boat and thought about Jesus and how much they missed him.** Give each child a cup. Ask kids to lie on their backs with their feet within reach of the pool. Have them place the cups between their feet and dip the cups into the pool to try to catch ice cubes.

☆ ☆ ☆ ☆ ☆

Leader Tip

If you play this game outdoors on a hot day, place the wading pool in the shade. Wait until kids have their feet in the pool before putting in the ice so the ice doesn't melt before you have a chance to play the game!

See how many ice cubes kids can catch before their feet get too cold. While kids dry their feet with towels, read the rest of the story (John 21:4-14). Again let kids fish, but this time they can use their hands to hold the cups and catch as many ice cubes as possible. Discuss the following questions:

• **Which way was easier for you to catch ice cubes? Why?**

• **According to the Bible story, when did the disciples catch the most fish?**

Say: **When the disciples saw Jesus and listened to him, they caught so many fish! Jesus had died and was buried; then Jesus rose again! He showed himself to the disciples in the boat and proved that he was alive! Jesus died for us and rose again so we can live forever!**

Joseph and His Brothers

Topic: Joseph
Scripture: Genesis 37; 42–45
Game Overview: Kids will pretend to be Joseph or the brothers on a fast chase.

☆ ☆ ☆ ☆ ☆

Supplies: Bible
Preparation: None needed

Form two groups—Joseph and the brothers. Have groups line up facing each other, about four feet apart in the middle of the playing area.

Tell kids the story of Joseph's jealous brothers who "got" him first and threw him in a pit (Genesis 37). Later Joseph had a chance later to "get" his brothers (Genesis 42–45).

Explain that you'll call out either "Joseph" or "brother." If you call out "Joseph," that team chases the other back to its home base (the wall behind them). Any kids who are tagged will join the Joseph team for the next round. Those who make it safely back to the wall will remain a brother for the next round.

Call out either "Joseph" or "brother," and let the chase begin. Then gather kids in the starting formation and have them play again. Vary the name you call so kids won't know what to expect.

☆ ☆ ☆ ☆ ☆

After a few rounds, gather kids in a circle. Tell them how Joseph had the opportunity to go after his brothers, but he didn't. Joseph was kind and forgave them. Then discuss the following questions:

• **Why is it hard to be kind and forgiving to people who aren't kind and forgiving to us?**

• **How can you be kind and forgiving when others aren't?**

Say: **God helps us to be kind and forgiving, even when we don't feel like it. Be like Joseph!**

Out of the Pit

Topic: Joseph
Scripture: Genesis 37:12-36
Game Overview: Kids will play a game of reverse limbo.

✫ ✫ ✫ ✫ ✫

Supplies: Bible, one twenty-foot garden hose that's attached to itself to form a circle, cushions or pillows
Preparation: None needed

Gather kids in a circle around the hose. Read Genesis 37:12-36 about how Joseph's jealous brothers threw him into a pit. Tell kids that they'll play a game and imagine they're in the pit with Joseph.

> ### Leader Tip
> Instead of using a garden hose, use a twenty-foot length of rope or bandannas tied together.

Choose one person to be Joseph and stand in the center of the circled hose. The rest of the kids will hold onto the hose. Kids will play this game as a reverse version of limbo, going over instead of under the hose. Ask kids to start by holding the hose at knee height to see whether Joseph can get out of the pit without touching it. Each time Joseph clears the hose without touching it, have kids raise the hose a few inches. As the hose gets higher, lay cushions on the ground and ask two kids to be spotters to ensure Joseph's safety. Allow Joseph to hold onto the shoulders of the hose holders and step onto their bent knees as he or she attempts to clear the pit. When Joseph touches the hose, have him or her choose the next Joseph.

✫ ✫ ✫ ✫ ✫

Be sure that everyone who wants to be Joseph gets a chance. Then have kids lay down the hose and discuss the following questions:

> ### Leader Tip
> To ensure Joseph's safety, don't let the hose get above shoulder height.

• **How did you feel playing this game?**
• **How do you think Joseph felt when he was in the pit? outside of it?**
Say: **Although things looked bad for Joseph at first, eventually he became an important leader and saved people's lives. Joseph forgave his brothers, too.**

Don't Get Ripped Off!

Topic: Joy

Scripture: John 15:9-11

Game Overview: Kids will take beanbags away from a blindfolded person and think of things that can "steal" a person's joy.

☆ ☆ ☆ ☆ ☆

Supplies: Bible, three beanbags, blindfold, name tags (one per child)

Preparation: Label each beanbag "joy." On separate name tags write "worry," "anger," "jealousy," "fear," or "lack of sleep," and other "joy stealers." Set the beanbags on a table.

Ask for four volunteers. Ask one of the volunteers to sit at the table with the beanbags near his or her hand, and blindfold the volunteer. Have the other three volunteers be "joy thieves" who'll try to steal the beanbags. Give each thief a name tag labeled "worry," "anger," "jealousy," "fear," "lack of sleep" or anything else that steals joy.

Each thief will get thirty seconds to steal a beanbag. As the first two thieves try, the blindfolded child may stop the thieves only if he or she hears them coming. He or she can't touch the beanbags. To stop the thief, the blindfolded child must listen carefully, then point and yell, "Stop thief!" The blindfolded child has three chances to point and yell at each of the first two thieves. For the third thief, allow the blindfolded child to rest one hand against the remaining beanbag(s). If the child feels a beanbag move, he or she may stop the thief.

☆ ☆ ☆ ☆ ☆

Let children take turns playing the different roles. At the end of the game, discuss the following questions:

• **What was it like for you to play this game?**

• **What things steal our joy in real life?**

Read John 15:9-11; then ask:

• **What brings joy to us?**

Say: **When we remember Jesus loves us and we obey what he tells us to do, joy stays inside us. Always remember Jesus loves you!**

Laugh Out Loud

Topic: Joy

Scripture: Psalm 126:2-3

Game Overview: Kids will laugh a special word as they find group members.

☆ ☆ ☆ ☆ ☆

Supplies: Bible

Preparation: None needed

Have kids number off by saying "ha," "hee," and "ho" instead of "one," "two," and "three." Mix the group by having kids close their eyes and turn three circles in place. Say: **When I say, "Laugh out loud," each one of you will find your group by saying the special word "ha," "hee," or "ho." When you've located another person, join hands and find the rest of your group. Ready? Laugh out loud!**

When all group members have found one another, challenge each group to say their laughter word, "ha," "hee," or "ho," ten times with straight faces. Allow the other groups to make silly faces to get kids to laugh.

☆ ☆ ☆ ☆ ☆

At the end of the game, discuss the following questions:

- **What was fun about this game?**
- **How did you get others to laugh?**
- **What makes you joyful each day?**

Read Psalm 126:2-3; then ask:

- **What made the person who wrote this psalm joyful?**
- **What "great things" has God blessed you with?**

Ask children to each share a blessing that gives them joy. Then go around the room, give kids high fives, and tell them they give you joy!

Danglin' Donuts

Topic: Joy

Scripture: Romans 12:12

Game Overview: Kids will dangle donuts in front of their partners, who'll try to eat the goodies.

☆ ☆ ☆ ☆ ☆

Supplies: Bible, donuts, string, scissors, newspapers, watch with a second hand, cups of chilled apple cider (one per child)

Preparation: Cut a twenty-four-inch piece of string for each child. Tie a donut to one end of each string.

Invite kids to form pairs and decide who'll be the first "donut dangler" and who'll be the first "donut chaser." Hand each pair a sheet of newspaper (crumb catcher) and two donuts on strings. Direct the donut chasers to kneel on the newspapers with their hands clasped behind their backs. Have the donut danglers dangle a donut in front of each chaser. Encourage the donut chasers to gobble as much of their donuts as possible in one minute. If donuts fall off the strings, have partners set their donuts aside and wait until you call time. At the end of one minute, have partners switch roles and then dangle and eat the other donuts.

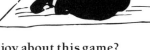

☆ ☆ ☆ ☆ ☆

When you've finished with the game, let kids finish their donuts and enjoy chilled apple cider. As you enjoy the snack, discuss the following questions:

- **What did you enjoy about this game?**
- **What was hard about this game?**

Read aloud Romans 12:12; then say: **It was kind of hard when we were on our knees trying to get the donuts, but we were having a good time doing it! The Bible tells us to be joyful and patient when times are hard. And just as we got to eat and drink a yummy snack, God has good plans for us. God loves us and cares for us through the hard times.**

Kindness Croquet

Topic: Kindness

Scripture: 1 Corinthians 13:4a

Game Overview: Kids will show kindness through their words and actions as they play croquet with human wickets.

☆ ☆ ☆ ☆ ☆

Supplies: Bible, softball or beach ball
Preparation: None needed

Set up a human croquet course, having kids act as the wickets. Set up a simple course based on how many kids you have. You'll want at least two children to be players at all times.

When you've set up your course, explain that no one will compete to beat anyone else in this game. The purpose is to show kindness through words and actions and to help everyone win. So as a child kicks the ball toward a "wicket," that wicket should move to let the ball go through it if it's at all possible. Have players take turns, one kick per turn, until they get the ball all the way through the course. Encourage kids throughout the playing time to show kindness in their words as well as their actions. Then have players change places with the wickets. Keep playing until everyone has had a chance to be both a wicket and a player.

☆ ☆ ☆ ☆ ☆

At the end of the game, discuss the following questions:

• **What kind actions and words did you use during the game?**

• **How was someone kind to you?**

Read 1 Corinthians 13:4a; then ask:

• **How do we show love to others by being kind to them?**

Ask kids to show kindness to one another by helping one another stand up, then giving one another back rubs, and playing the game again.

Leader Tip

If you have more than twenty-four kids, have two kids stand facing each other and join hands to form each wicket. If you have twelve to twenty-four kids, have one child form each wicket by standing with feet apart, or by kneeling on hands and knees.

Build Up Buddies

MEDIUM ★★★★★ ENERGY

Topic: Kindness

Scripture: 1 Thessalonians 5:11

Game Overview: Kids will build up one another with kind words as they stuff a shirt with balloons.

★ ★ ★ ★ ★

Supplies: Bible, grocery sacks (one for each group of six), extra-large men's sweatshirts (one for each group of six), balloons (about fifteen for each group of six)

Preparation: Ask volunteers to help you inflate and tie the balloons. Put fifteen balloons in each sack (for groups of six).

Have kids form groups of no more than six, and give each group a sack of balloons. Read aloud 1 Thessalonians 5:11, and ask groups to each choose one person to "build up." Have those chosen put on large sweatshirts.

Say: **Let's pretend each balloon represents a kind word. Your group members will fill the sweatshirts with kind words. You'll have one minute to stuff the shirt with kind words. Ready? Go!**

After a minute, call time and have the built-up volunteers parade around the room. Have the groups return the balloons to the sacks.

★ ★ ★ ★ ★

Have everyone sit down in a circle, and discuss the following questions:

• **What happened when you stuffed the shirts with kind words?**

• **What happens when we fill people with kind words and actions?**

Say: **God helps us to be kind and build up others.**

Crowd Around

Topic: Loving others

Scripture: 1 John 4:7-12

Game Overview: Kids will show loving actions as they crowd onto different sections of a playing area.

☆ ☆ ☆ ☆ ☆

Supplies: Bible, masking tape, scissors, four different colors of butcher paper (such as yellow, red, blue, and orange)

Preparation: For each group of eight to ten kids, make a game board as follows: Cut a 4x4-foot section of each color of butcher paper. Tape the four colors to the floor to form a square.

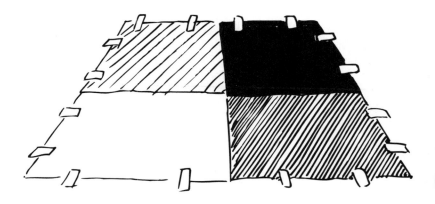

Read 1 John 4:7-12; then say: **Wow! God says we're supposed to love one another because love comes from God! Let's play a game and show love to others.**

Ask each eight to ten kids to stand around a game board. Tell kids to stand in a crowd on the color you'll say and do the loving action that you call out:

- **Stand on yellow. Give three people high fives and say your name.**
- **Stand on red. Give two people a shoulder rub.**
- **Stand on blue. Tell two people what you like about them.**
- **Stand on orange. Give one person a handshake as you say, "God loves you and so do I."**

Continue calling out colors and loving actions, such as "Pat as many backs as you can until the leader counts to ten." Every now and then, call out a color that kids are already standing on.

☆ ☆ ☆ ☆ ☆

At the end of the game, have everyone sit around one of the game boards. Discuss these questions:

- **What loving actions did you show others in this game?**
- **Why does God want us to love others?**
- **How can you show God's love to someone when you go home?**

Say: **God wants us to love others because God is love and he wants people to know about it.** Call out one more action: **Stand any place on this game board, and everyone give me a hug!**

Chicken

Topic: Loving others

Scripture: John 13:34-35

Game Overview: Kids will play a Hopscotch-type game from China.

☆ ☆ ☆ ☆ ☆

Supplies: Bible

Preparation: None needed

Have players each remove one shoe. Place the shoes in a straight line about one foot apart. The first player will hop on his or her shoed foot over each of the shoes in the line. When the player gets to the last shoe, the player will kick that shoe out of line, turn, and hop back over the remaining shoes. If the player puts both feet on the ground at any time, a second player will take over at that place. The game will continue in the same manner until kids kick all the shoes out of place. Then again line up the shoes so everyone gets a turn.

The next time kids play, form partners and have partners help each other play the game. One person will be the "hopper," and the other will be the "loving helper." As the hopper hops the course, the loving helper will show loving actions such as supporting the hopper as that person hops or starts to fall, helping move shoes, saying encouraging words, and so on.

☆ ☆ ☆ ☆ ☆

At the end of the game, have kids put on their shoes. Then discuss these questions:

• **What was it like to play the game the first time? the second time?**

• **How did you show love through your actions? your words?**

Read John 13:34-35; then ask:

• **Why should we love others?**

Say: **Jesus gave us a new command to love one another, just as he loves us. People know we love Jesus if we love one another.**

Love Launch

Topic: Loving others

Scripture: 1 John 4:19

Game Overview: Kids will use a unique scoop to catch a ball.

☆ ☆ ☆ ☆ ☆

Supplies: Bible, scissors, tennis balls (one for every six kids), empty plastic milk jugs (one for every child)

Preparation: Cut each milk jug around the middle about two inches below the handle. Discard the bottom half. The remaining half will form a plastic scoop kids will use to catch balls. You'll need one scoop for each child.

Give each child a plastic scoop, and have kids form teams of up to six kids. Give each team one tennis ball, and say: **Use your scoop to toss the tennis ball high into the air. Another team member will catch it in his or her scoop.** Demonstrate how to do this. **Before you toss the ball, tell of one way you can show love to others. For example, before you fling the ball into the air, you might say, "Smile and be helpful."**

☆ ☆ ☆ ☆ ☆

Begin the game. Encourage team members to take turns throwing and catching the balls. After kids have played several minutes, gather all the scoops and balls. Then discuss the following question:

• **What loving actions did you think of?**

Read 1 John 4:19; then ask:

• **According to this verse, why should we love others?**

Say: **Jesus wants us to love others, because he first loved us!**

Water Flows Downhill

LOW ENERGY

Topic: Moses

Scripture: Exodus 15:22-27

Game Overview: Kids will use paper plates to pass a golf ball.

☆ ☆ ☆ ☆ ☆

Supplies: Bible, golf ball, paper plates (one per child)

Preparation: None needed

Gather kids, and briefly tell the story of how the Israelites grumbled against Moses for water (Exodus 15:22-27). Say: **Poor Moses! The Israelites were thirsty from all that walking in the desert. They wanted water, and they wanted it now! Let's play a game to see how it feels to wait for something.**

Give each person a paper plate to crease in half to create a trough.

Line up children side by side. Ask them to roll a golf ball from plate to plate all the way down the line. Keep the line going by having each child move to the end of the line after the ball has rolled through that child's plate to the next plate. If the ball falls, have kids pick it up and start the ball at the beginning.

☆ ☆ ☆ ☆ ☆

At the end of the game, discuss the following questions:

• **What was it like to be at the end of the line and watch the ball come your way?**

• **Do you think the Israelites were patient when they were waiting for water? Why or why not?**

• **How did God help the Israelites in the Bible story?**

• **How does God help us today?**

Say: **God helped the Israelites, and God helps us. Let's always have patience and remember that God loves us and takes care of us.**

Manna from Heaven

Topic: Moses

Scripture: Exodus 16:1-26

Game Overview: Kids will flip and catch some tasty "manna."

★ ★ ★ ★ ★

Supplies: Bible, mini-marshmallows, plastic spoons, butcher paper

Preparation: Cover the floor with butcher paper so you can reuse marshmallow "manna" that falls. Ask children to wash their hands before playing.

Help kids form pairs. Summarize the story of God feeding the Israelites with manna from heaven (Exodus 16:1-26).

Ask pairs to sit on the butcher paper. Then give each pair a plastic spoon and eight mini-marshmallows (manna). Ask pairs to take turns flipping manna at each other. Kids can't use their hands to catch manna, only their mouths.

★ ★ ★ ★ ★

At the end of the game, discuss the following questions:

• **How would you feel if you had to rely on what fell from the sky for your food?**

• **How do you think God's people felt about relying on God for their food?**

• **How is that like or unlike you relying on God for your food?**

Remind kids to thankfully rely on God for good blessings, and then let kids eat and enjoy more mini-marshmallows!

Leader of the Crowd

Topic: Moses

Scripture: Exodus 13:17–15:21

Game Overview: Kids will act out the Israelites and the Egyptians as they race to the water.

☆ ☆ ☆ ☆ ☆

Supplies: Bible, two long lengths of rope, two chairs, sprinkler, hose and faucet

Preparation: Take the supplies outside to a large playing area. If you want to play inside, you'll have to play without the water!

Summarize the story of the Israelites crossing the Red Sea. Have kids form two groups: the Israelites and the Egyptians. Ask each group to hold hands to form a circle, then take three large steps backward. Place a chair in the middle of each circle. Set a sprinkler about twenty yards from both of the groups, and turn on the sprinkler. (See illustration.)

Choose one person from the Israelite group to be Moses and one person from the Egyptian group to be Pharaoh. Give one of the rope circles to Moses and the other to Pharaoh, and have them each stand in the middle of their groups.

Say: **Moses, it's your job to gather your people as fast as you can to cross the Red Sea. You'll gather your people by running from the chair to one person. Have that person get inside the rope with you and run back to the chair. You'll then run together to another person, and have him or her get inside the rope. Then the three of you**

> ## Leader Tip
> Kids will play in two teams, so each team will need one rope. You'll need about two feet of rope for every child who's supposed to fit inside it.

Chair · Rope · Rope · chair · Sprinkler→

will run back to the chair in the middle. Continue this process until all of the Israelites have gathered inside the rope. When they've all gathered, run to the chair one last time, then run with your group across the sprinkler—which is the Red Sea.

Pharaoh will gather the Egyptians in the same way and will try to lead his group through the Red Sea before Moses and the Israelites get there. Ready? Let's play!

✮ ✮ ✮ ✮ ✮

At the end of the game, discuss the following questions:

• How do you think the Israelites felt as the Egyptians chased them?
• How did God show the Israelites that he loved them?

Say: **God saved the Israelites from the Egyptians because he loved them. God loves us and save us, too.**

Bang the Bucket

Topic: Obedience

Scripture: 1 John 5:1-3

Game Overview: Kids will obey directions as they form and then re-form trios.

☆ ☆ ☆ ☆ ☆

Supplies: Metal bucket or sturdy metal wastebasket, wooden spoon, watch with second hand

Preparation: None needed

Ask kids to form trios. Say: **Every time I bang the bucket, you'll have twenty seconds to form a new trio—with different people. Then you'll have forty-five seconds to discuss the question I ask. Follow my orders every time I bang the bucket!**

Ask the discussion starters, giving trios approximately forty-five seconds to talk before you again bang the bucket.

- **What's the weirdest haircut you've seen?**
- **Tell about your favorite socks.**
- **Imitate a cartoon character.**
- **Describe with a sound how much you like math.**
- **Explain your answer to this question: Would you rather have a broken toe or a broken finger?**

☆ ☆ ☆ ☆ ☆

At the end of the game, bang the bucket one more time and tell kids to sit in a circle. Discuss the following questions:

- **Who was in charge of this game? Why?**
- **You didn't have to obey me each time, but you did. Why?**
- **This game was far more fun when you obeyed the leader. In what ways are our lives more fun when we obey Jesus?**

Bang the bucket again, and have kids tell two people, "Obey Jesus."

The Big Fish

Topic: Obedience

Scripture: Jonah 1–4

Game Overview: Kids will listen carefully and obey instructions in this fast-paced game.

✫ ✫ ✫ ✫ ✫

Supplies: Bible, three sheets of construction paper, marker, tape, two blankets

Preparation: Label one sheet of construction paper "Joppa," another "Tarshish," and the other "Nineveh." Tape the three sheets in three different areas of your room—far enough apart so kids will have to run between the cities. Place one blanket at Tarshish and another one at Joppa.

Review the story of Jonah (Jonah 1–4); then play this game.

Select one player to be the "big fish." Say: **All the rest of you are now Jonahs, and you're in danger of being grabbed by the big fish! When I yell "Joppa," you must run to Joppa to be safe.** Point to the area with the Joppa sign. **Everyone who makes it safely to Joppa will hide under the blanket until you hear me call another city. When I yell "Tarshish," you must run to Tarshish to be safe.** Point to the area with the Tarshish sign. **Everyone who makes it safely to Tarshish will hide under the blanket. When I call "Nineveh," you must run to Nineveh to be safe.** Point to the area with the Nineveh sign. **You'll have no blanket to hide under there because when Jonah finally went to Nineveh, he obeyed God. So when you get to Nineveh, you'll say, "Obey God." If I call, "Man overboard," you may run to any city you want.**

Each time I call a new city, you must avoid getting tagged by the big fish. If you do get tagged, you'll become a big fish and help tag others.

✫ ✫ ✫ ✫ ✫

Play a couple times, and stop playing when kids need to catch their breath. Gather in the

Leader Tip

To make the game more interesting and more realistic, place Joppa and Nineveh fairly close together and Tarshish farther away. Talk with the kids about how Jonah would have been safe traveling the short distance to Nineveh as God had commanded, but instead he chose to flee to Tarshish, which was clear across the Mediterranean Sea!

Nineveh location, and discuss the following questions:

- Why didn't Jonah want to obey God?
- What happened when Jonah disobeyed God?
- What happened when Jonah finally obeyed God?
- How does God want us to obey him?

Say: **God wants us to obey his teachings. God wants everyone to know that Jesus died for us. Because of Jesus, we'll live forever.**

Prayer Square Twist

Topic: Prayer

Scripture: 1 Thessalonians 5:16-18

Game Overview: Kids will dance, pray, and praise on carpet prayer squares.

✮ ✮ ✮ ✮ ✮

Supplies: Bible, carpet squares (one per child), CD player, Christian music, chalk, chalkboard

Preparation: Meet in a room with a wood or tile floor. Ask two teenagers or adults to help record prayers of thanksgivings during the game.

Give each child a carpet square, and have kids stand an arm's length from one another. Ask them to put their carpet square pile-side down on the floor.

Read 1 Thessalonians 5:16-18; then say: **The Bible says to be joyful, pray always, and give thanks anywhere we are. Let's do all these things as we play a game and call out a long list of things we're thankful for.**

Asks the two volunteers to stand by the chalkboard and be ready to record all the things kids say they're thankful for. Have them use tally marks if kids say the same thing more than once.

Play the CD, and have kids stand on their squares and twist to the music. Every now and then, stop the CD and have kids shout out one-word prayers of thanksgivings such as "food," "family," "friends," "church," and "pets." When you start the CD again, kids must move to a new square and twist to the music. Continue until kids have danced joyfully on several different carpet squares and shouted out a long list of thanksgivings.

✮ ✮ ✮ ✮ ✮

At the end of the game, have kids move their prayer squares into a circle and sit on them. Discuss the following questions:

• **Why do you think God wants us to pray and give thanks always?**

• **What other prayers of thanksgiving can you give to God?** Have the volunteers add these to the chalkboard list as well.

Say: **Look at our long list of things we're thankful for! Our good God loves us and has blessed us so much. Remember what the Bible tells us: Be joyful, pray always, and give thanks anywhere we are!**

Turn on the CD again, and once more have kids dance on their squares. Keep the squares in your room, and use them regularly for praising, praying, and for just having a spot to sit on!

Alone or Together

Topic: Prayer

Scripture: Luke 5:16

Game Overview: Kids will play a form of Hide-and-Seek and then pray alone and as a big group.

☆ ☆ ☆ ☆ ☆

Supplies: Bible

Preparation: None needed

Play a version of Hide-and-Seek. Ask kids to cover their eyes while another person finds a place to hide. On your command, have kids search for the hidden person. When a child has discovered the hidden person, he or she will stay there quietly until everyone has found the spot and has crowded together.

After one round of the game, ask everyone to sit in a circle. Say: **We can pray to God anytime and anyplace. We can pray when we're alone or when we're in a big crowd. Let's play the game one more time, but this time we'll play and pray!**

Ask kids to cover their eyes while another person hides. Have all the kids say a silent prayer to God while they're in this solitary position. Then have kids search for the hidden person. As they find the hidden person, they will stay there until everyone has crowded into the same spot. Then have the crowd of kids say a prayer together, such as "Thanks, God, for each person here!"

☆ ☆ ☆ ☆ ☆

When kids have finished the game, discuss the following questions:
- **What was it like to pray alone? as a large group?**
- **When do you pray each day?**
- **How do you pray?**

Read aloud Luke 5:16; then ask:
- **When did Jesus pray?**

Say: **Jesus prayed all the time. He prayed when he was alone, and he prayed as he did miracles with large crowds of people. We can be like Jesus and pray all the time, too.**

Move 'em Out

Topic: School

Scripture: Philippians 4:6-7

Game Overview: Kids will use index cards to transport goodies to a bowl.

✮ ✮ ✮ ✮ ✰

Supplies: Bible, four bowls, Oreo cookies, and index cards (one per child)

Preparation: Place Oreo cookies in two bowls, and place the bowls close to one wall. Set the two other bowls about ten feet from the cookie-filled bowls.

Ask kids to form two lines behind the cookie-filled bowls. Give each child an index card. Say: **At times, we may face some problems when we go to school. But Jesus always helps us with our problems. Let's play a game in which we'll get to eat something good in the end. The problem right now is that you have to carry the goodies by using only the index card, which you'll place in your mouth.**

Demonstrate how to put the index card in your mouth, and then take a cookie from the bowl and place it on the index card. Run to the opposite empty bowl and drop the cookie in it.

✮ ✮ ✮ ✮ ✰

After each child has had a turn, reward kids with the cookies. Then read aloud Philippians 4:6-7, and discuss the following questions:

· **What was difficult about this game?**

· **What hard things do you face in real life? at school?**

· **How does Jesus help you in those hard times?**

Say: **When we worry about problems we may face at school or anywhere, God wants us to pray with thanks and we'll feel peace.**

Worry Whirl

Topic: School

Scripture: Jeremiah 29:11

Game Overview: Kids will whirl around the room with a partner.

☆ ☆ ☆ ☆ ☆

Supplies: Bible, blindfolds (one for every two children)

Preparation: None needed

Have kids form pairs and discuss this question:

• **What's one thing you worry about with school?**

Have pairs decide which partner would like to be blindfolded first during this game. Distribute the blindfolds, and have kids put them on.

Have pairs link arms back to back and line up at one end of your meeting room. Say: **When I say, "Worry whirl," think about your school worries as you race to the opposite wall and back. You won't just walk or run to the wall, but you'll spin around in circles with your partner as you race. Seeing partners, you're responsible for the welfare of your blindfolded partners. Ready? Worry whirl!**

Run the race, and then have partners switch roles and race again.

☆ ☆ ☆ ☆ ☆

At the end of the game, discuss the following questions:

• **How did you feel when you played this game?**

• **How is that like when you worry about school?**

Read Jeremiah 29:11; then say: **Sometimes we feel as if we're spinning around with our worries. But God wants us to trust him. God has good plans for us. God is in control.**

School Moves and Sounds

Topic: School

Scripture: Luke 2:40, 46-47

Game Overview: Kids will pantomime and make school sound effects.

☆ ☆ ☆ ☆ ☆

Supplies: Bible

Preparation: None needed

Ask the kids to sit in a circle. Read Luke 2:40, 46-47, and tell kids about Jesus growing up, learning from his carpenter father Joseph, and going to the temple and astonishing some grown men with his wisdom. Say that just as Jesus grew and learned, they're growing and learning, too.

Ask kids to think of skills they're learning at school. One at a time, have kids act out skills while the others guess. For example, a child could pretend to write, read, kick a ball, or sing.

Say: **Wow! You're learning so many things. All of those actions are making me think of school memories. In a minute, I'll say something you might hear at school. Then you'll make sounds like the thing I tell you.**

Tell kids they may use only their voices and their bodies (slapping knees, clapping, stomping feet) to produce the given sounds. Here are some "sound" ideas: first-graders after hearing they get an extra recess, preschoolers at a day-care playground, school buses warming up their engines in the school parking lot, kids racing through the halls on the last day of school.

Say: **What good school memories. Those sounds brought it all back. Just as Jesus grew in wisdom, you are too. Jesus is with you at school and wherever you go!**

Wrapped-Up Relay

Topic: Service
Scripture: John 13:1-9
Game Overview: Kids will serve others as they run a relay.

☆ ☆ ☆ ☆ ☆

Supplies: Bible, toilet paper, masking tape, watch with a second hand
Preparation: Create two parallel masking tape lines on the floor, fifteen feet apart.

Help kids form two teams. Have them stand behind one of the lines, facing the other line.

Tell kids that each team member will run, one at a time, to the far line and back. No one may run until both feet are completely wrapped in toilet tissue—each foot separately, not together. Only one person in each team may have both feet wrapped at any time.

Give each team a roll of toilet paper. Encourage kids to help one another wrap the first runner's feet. When that runner has run to the other line and back, encourage kids to help the next runner wrap his or her feet. While the second runner runs, kids will help the first runner unwrap his or her feet.

Run the relay twice, encouraging teams to improve on their times.

☆ ☆ ☆ ☆ ☆

At the end of the game, gather the kids and read John 13:1-9. Then ask:

> ## Leader Tip
> Make sure the playing surface isn't slippery. Safety first!

• When you helped one another, the job of wrapping feet went faster. How does serving others make life easier?

• Jesus washed his disciples' feet. What can we do to serve others?

Say: Jesus asks us to serve others—but he served us, too, by dying in our place so we can come to God. Jesus is the best servant!

Mitten Outreach

Topic: Service

Scripture: Matthew 25:31-46

Game Overview: Kids will wear mittens as they organize them to give away.

☆ ☆ ☆ ☆ ☆

Supplies: Bible, mittens, tissue, boxes, markers

Preparation: Encourage your kids to work with the church to organize an outreach for people who need help. If it's winter, your church might have a mitten drive to collect mittens for children in your area who need them. At other times, have your church collect gloves, such as bike gloves, baseball gloves, batting gloves, catcher's mitts, and so on.

Gather kids to organize the mittens collected in the drive. Play a game with the mittens while you're at it.

Ask everyone to put on a pair of mittens or gloves. Then set out the supplies, and have kids wear the mittens as they do the following:

- Divide the mittens according to size.
- Place tissue paper in the boxes.
- Place like mittens in each box.
- Count the number of mittens in each box.
- Take off the mittens they're working in and place them in the appropriate box.
- Label each box with the number and type of mittens inside.

☆ ☆ ☆ ☆ ☆

> ## Leader Tip
>
> Time the kids as they do each of the tasks. Then at the end, total the minutes it took to organize the outreach. Encourage kids to give one another many pats on the back for a job well done!

At the end of the organizing, discuss the following questions:

- **What was easy or hard about this activity?**
- **How might that be like being in need?**

Briefly summarize for kids the parable of the sheep and the goats (Matthew 25:31-46). Read aloud verse 40. Then say: **Whatever you do for people in need, you're doing for Jesus.**

Ask kids and their parents to car pool with you to deliver the mittens to an outreach center.

Recycling Fun

Topic: Service

Scripture: Genesis 1:28b

Game Overview: Kids will collect cans and play a game before recycling them.

☆ ☆ ☆ ☆ ☆

Supplies: Bible, empty aluminum cans

Preparation: The next time you collect aluminum cans for recycling, play this game before smashing the cans.

Tell kids that they'll work together to build the biggest pyramid possible with the cans. Show them how to use more cans on the bottom row, then one fewer for each new row. All the cans must be upright. Then have kids race to see how quickly they can smash and bag (or box) all the cans!

☆ ☆ ☆ ☆ ☆

At the end of the game, read Genesis 1:28b. Then discuss the following questions:

• **What does the Bible say we're responsible for taking care of?**

• **How does recycling help take care of God's earth?**

Compliment the kids on all their help, and then remember to deliver the cans to a recycling center.

> **Leader Tip**
>
> Rinse out the cans and drain them so nothing spills during the game.

Spinning With Good News

Topic: Sharing faith

Scripture: Acts 13:47-49

Game Overview: Kids will roll on a swivel chair and tell good news.

★ ★ ★ ★ ☆

Supplies: Bible, swivel chair with wheels

Preparation: None needed

Ask the kids to sit in a circle. Read Acts 13:47-49; then ask:

• **What's some good news you know about Jesus?**

Roll a swivel chair into the center of the circle. Ask for a volunteer to sit in the swivel chair. Instruct two others to roll the chair around the circle while the volunteer shouts out some good news about Jesus, such as "Jesus loves you!" Have the volunteer say it so each person in the circle hears it as he or she rolls around the circle.

Let another child sit in the chair while two others roll him or her around the circle. Have the new child shout out more good news.

★ ★ ★ ★ ☆

Let everyone have a turn on the chair, and then have kids answer these questions:

• **What good news did you share about Jesus?**

• **How did the two people help you share your good news?**

• **How can we help one another tell the world about Jesus?**

Say: **We have so much good news to tell the world about Jesus. Let's help one another spread the word about Jesus and his awesome love!**

The Great Hunt

Topic: Sharing faith

Scripture: Psalm 64:9

Game Overview: Kids will find others by matching parts of a candy bar, then create a cheer about why their goodie is the best.

★ ★ ★ ★ ★

Supplies: Bible, resealable snack bags, candy bars, knife, box, tape, paper

Preparation: Cut different kinds of candy bars in half so that you have four similar pieces of candy. Place each piece in a separate snack bag. Put all the bags of candy bar pieces in a box that doesn't allow kids to see which bag they select when the game begins. Tape each candy bar wrapper to a sheet of paper to make a sign, and place the signs around the room.

Pass around the box and let kids draw out a snack bag. Tell kids to find the matching pieces of the candy bar. When they've found the matching pieces, they should go to the sign for their candy bar and as a team make up a cheer about why their candy bar is the best. For example, a group may say, "Snickers. Snickers. They're so filling. We keep eating and the dentist keeps drilling." After five minutes, call on each candy bar team to give their individual names and their cheers. After kids have finished all the cheers, let the kids eat their candy bars.

Say: **Great job with the cheers and telling us why your candy bar is the best. Since you did such a good job with that, make up one more cheer with your team. In this cheer, tell us about Jesus and why he's the best! For example, you could cheer, "Jesus, Jesus, he's so cool. Believe in him 'cause he will rule!"**

After each team cheers for Jesus, have everyone applaud and then have them gather in the center of the room. By the end of all the cheers, you'll have one group of people sitting together.

★ ★ ★ ★ ★

Read Psalm 64:9; then discuss the following questions:
- **What things did we tell about Jesus in our cheers?**
- **Who can you tell about Jesus?**
- **What will you say about Jesus?**

Say: **Let's shout for joy and tell everyone about Jesus and how much he loves us. Jesus is great!**

Drip Drop

Topic: Sin and salvation

Scripture: Romans 8:21-25a

Game Overview: Kids will aim for a small target and get a little wet.

☆ ☆ ☆ ☆ ☆

Supplies: Bible, two paper cups, a large bowl of water, two tablespoons, a towel, a tarp

Preparation: Lay out a tarp and set the supplies on it, or play outside.

ave kids form two teams and gather by the supplies. Ask each team to choose one person to lie on the floor with a cup balanced on his or her forehead. While standing straight up, team members will take turns dipping a tablespoon into the bowl of water, then pouring the water into the cup on their team member's forehead. Encourage teams to try to get as much water into their cups as possible.

Let everyone have a chance to balance a cup on his or her head and get a little wet.

☆ ☆ ☆ ☆ ☆

At the end of the game, discuss the following question:

• **How easy or hard was it for you to get the water into the cup?**

Read Romans 8:21-25a; then ask:

• **According to this verse, how easy or hard is it to stop sinning?**

• **According to this verse, what does Jesus do?**

Say: **Jesus saves us from our sins. Kind of like the person who took all our spills when we were trying to get water in the cup, Jesus took our sins with him to the cross. Jesus saves us from the bad things we do and helps us do what's right.**

Release the Captive

Topic: Sin and salvation

Scripture: Luke 19:10

Game Overview: Kids will play a game and attempt to snatch away a sock.

☆ ☆ ☆ ☆ ☆

Supplies: Bible, socks (one for every six to eight kids)

Preparation: None needed

Form teams of six to eight kids, and have each team form a circle. Give a sock to one child in each team to tuck into the neckline of his or her T-shirt. Make sure the sock can be easily removed. Ask the child with the sock to stand inside the circle, and ask the other kids to turn away from the child in the circle and stand close together to form a protective wall. Ask another child to stand outside the circle.

The goal is for the child outside the circle to nab the sock. The kids will stand close together and try to block the outside child from nabbing the sock from the inside child's shirt. When the outside child has nabbed the sock, have kids switch roles and play again.

☆ ☆ ☆ ☆ ☆

At the end of the game, discuss the following questions:

• **How did you feel when you were trying to save the sock?**

• **How is that like Jesus coming to save us from sin?**

Read aloud Luke 19:10; then say: **The Bible tells us Jesus came to seek and to save the lost. Jesus saved us from our sins!**

Turtle Relay

Topic: Sin and salvation

Scripture: John 12:46

Game Overview: Kids will race while wearing boxes, race without the boxes, and then compare the game to sin and forgiveness.

☆ ☆ ☆ ☆ ☆

Supplies: Bible, two appliance boxes, stopwatch

Preparation: Halfway up one side of each box, cut a hole big enough for a child to stick his or her head through. Then cut out the bottom of each box.

Ask kids to line up along one wall. Have kids form two relay teams, and give each team a box. Say: **The object is for you to run a relay like turtles. The first people in each line will wear this "shell," crawl to the opposite wall, then return to tag the next teammate. The next person should put on the shell, crawl to the wall and back, and tag the next person. You'll repeat this until the whole team has raced in the shell. Ready? Go!**

Time kids as they crawl through the race. Then play the game again, but this time have kids run without the shells. Time this race, and compare the two times.

☆ ☆ ☆ ☆ ☆

At the end of the game, discuss the following questions:

• **What was it like to crawl while wearing a shell for the relay?**

• **How is this like sin in our lives?**

• **What was it like to run without the shell?**

• **How is this like Jesus' forgiveness?**

Read John 12:46; then say: **Jesus' forgiveness gets us out of the shell of darkness. Thank God for sending Jesus to save us from our sins!**

Hannah's Hot Seat

Topic: Thankfulness

Scripture: 1 Samuel 2:1

Game Overview: Kids will find a heart and give thanks.

★ ★ ★ ★ ★

Supplies: Bible, chairs (one per person), CD player, upbeat Christian music, tape, red construction paper, scissors

Preparation: Set the chairs in a circle. Cut three hearts from the construction paper, and tape them underneath the seats of three chairs.

Read 1 Samuel 2:1, and say: **Hannah was so thankful when God answered her prayer that she gave her son back to God. We can express our praises in lots of ways.** Let's play a game to tell a few of the things we're thankful for.

Play upbeat Christian music, and instruct kids to move around the circle of chairs in a wacky way, such as hopping, skipping, walking backward, tiptoeing, or taking giant steps. Have everyone move in the same fashion.

After a few seconds, stop the music and instruct everyone to take a seat as quickly as possible. Kids might be surprised to discover enough seats for everyone.

Say: **Look under your seat. If you see a paper heart, you're in the "hot seat." Shout out one thing you're thankful for.** Pause while kids share their thanks. Then say: **Now, everyone close your eyes and stay seated while the people in the hot seats move the hearts to different chairs.** Pause while kids sneak around and move the hearts. When they've returned to their seats, play the music and have kids play again. Continue until all kids have had a chance to share.

Say: **God helps us to be thankful. Sometimes, it's good to just stop and remember all the terrific things God's given us. In fact, let's take a minute and thank him now.** Lead kids in a prayer similar to this one: **Dear God, thank you so much for all the things that have been mentioned in this game. Thanks for loving us and helping us change our world. In Jesus' name, amen.**

Leader Tip

Keep up the pace of this game and build excitement by suggesting wacky ways for kids to move around the chairs. For example, "Weave in and out," "Sit down, then stand up, sit down, then stand up" and so on. Kids may even have a few silly suggestions of their own!

Treasure Thanks

Topic: Thankfulness

Scripture: Matthew 6:19-21

Game Overview: Kids will search for pennies hidden around a room in the church and learn about spiritual treasures.

☆ ☆ ☆ ☆ ☆

Supplies: Bible, 100 pennies

Preparation: Hide the pennies throughout the room.

Tell kids that you've hidden pennies around the room. Count to three, and then have kids begin searching for the pennies. After three minutes, stop the game and have kids form a circle. Ask them each to name one thing they're thankful for, either physical or spiritual, for every penny they've found.

☆ ☆ ☆ ☆ ☆

After kids have shared what they're thankful for, read aloud Matthew 6:19-21; then ask:

• **What are things you're thankful for?**

• **What does the verse mean by "where your treasure is, there your heart will be also"?**

• **How does keeping our eyes on Jesus and all his blessings help us to be thankful?**

Say: **Let's always think about Jesus and keep him in our hearts. Jesus has blessed us with so many things that we can be thankful for.**

Thanks for the Pizza

Topic: Thankfulness

Scripture: Psalm 136:1

Game Overview: Kids will nibble pieces of pizza into shapes of things they're thankful for.

☆ ☆ ☆ ☆ ☆

Supplies: Bible, pizza, napkins, drinks

Preparation: Order or bake pizza, and set out the goodies.

Hand out one slice of pizza to each player, and have kids try to nibble their pizza slices into shapes of things for which they're thankful, such as a cross for Jesus, a heart for love of a parent, a star for being a good soccer player, and so on. When kids have finished nibbling, ask:

• **What are you thankful for?**

Then let each child show his or her tasty symbol.

Read Psalm 136:1; then say: **Not only is this pizza good, but God is good. He loves us forever. Let's always give thanks to our good God!**

Say a prayer of thanks, and let kids eat and drink more of the goodies.

Great Impressions

Topic: Truthfulness

Scripture: Proverbs 23:23

Game Overview: Kids will use Silly Putty or Play-Doh to make impressions of objects they find around the church. Then they won't tell which objects have made the impressions.

☆ ☆ ☆ ☆ ☆

Supplies: Bible, Silly Putty or Play-Doh (enough for each child to have a small piece)

Preparation: None needed

Give each child a piece of Silly Putty or Play-Doh. Then ask kids to leave the room and each make an impression of something in the church.

For example, the tread from the bottom of the pastor's shoe, the words on the cover of a Bible, or the grating on a heating vent.

Have kids bring back their impressions and get ready to tell about them. Say: **One at a time, show what you've found. While others guess what it is, hide the truth from us and don't say anything. Don't tell us what it is until everyone has guessed.**

☆ ☆ ☆ ☆ ☆

After kids have finally guessed the truth, discuss the following questions:

• **What was it like to hide the truth from us?**

• **What was it like to finally tell the truth?**

Read Proverbs 23:23; then say: **The Bible says truth is so important we need to buy it and not sell it. It's important to be truthful with our friends, family, and everyone.**

Play the game again, but this time have kids tell right away about their impressions.

To Tell the Truth

Topic: Truthfulness

Scripture: Proverbs 16:13

Game Overview: Kids will share three "facts" about themselves. Which is true? Which is false?

☆ ☆ ☆ ☆ ☆

Supplies: Bible

Preparation: None needed

Ask kids to sit in a circle and take turns sharing three "facts" about themselves—two true and one false. When kids have heard the three facts, they must hold up one, two, or three fingers to vote on which fact they think is false. After each vote, have kids reveal the correct answer.

Read Proverbs 16:13; then have kids pass this phrase around the circle: "Jesus takes pleasure in honest lips." After each child has said the phrase, he or she will kiss his or her hands and blow a kiss to the next person, who will repeat the phrase and blow a kiss, and so on around the circle.

☆ ☆ ☆ ☆ ☆

At the end of the game, discuss these questions:
- **Why should we tell the truth and not lies?**
- **How do you feel when someone lies to you?**

Say: **Sometimes people say things that aren't true. But we can always trust God's promises! God never lies!**

Upper Elementary Games

Paul wrote to Timothy, "Don't let anyone look down on you because you are young, but set an example for the believers in speech, in life, in love, in faith and purity" (1 Timothy 4:12). True words of encouragement from a mentor of the faith! You are a "Paul" to your young "Timothys." Fourth- through sixth-graders are rapidly growing both physically and spiritually. What better way to teach them in speech, life, love, faith, and purity than in the church!

Use the games in this section to encourage and "be there" as a mentor for upper elementary kids. All games are noncompetitive, and they contain questions and Scripture references to stimulate lively discussions with these growing young Christians. When upper elementary kids play the games, they connect to real-life issues such as cliques, loving others, thankfulness, and telling others about Jesus.

Who Is That?

Topic: The Bible

Scripture: 2 Timothy 3:16-17; James 1:22-25

Game Overview: Kids will draw self-portraits while blindfolded.

☆ ☆ ☆ ☆ ☆

Supplies: Bible, paper, pencils, blindfolds

Preparation: None needed

Give each person a sheet of paper, a pencil, and a blindfold. After each player is blindfolded, have kids write the answers to the following questions:

- **What color are your socks?**
- **What color is your shirt?**
- **What is distinctive about the outfit you're wearing?**

After everyone has written answers to the questions, have kids turn over their papers, keeping their blindfolds on, and draw pictures of themselves. After three minutes, have kids take off the blindfolds and show their self-portraits.

☆ ☆ ☆ ☆ ☆

Next, give everyone another sheet of paper and have kids draw another self-portrait—this time while they can see. Compare the results of the two portraits, and discuss the following questions:

- **What was difficult about this game?**
- **What was the difference in the outcome when you could see?**
- **How is this like God's Word—the Bible?**

Say: **The Bible helps us see ourselves clearly. It tells us how God sees us, too. God loves each one of us!** Ask volunteers to read 2 Timothy 3:16-17 and James 1:22-25; then ask:

- **What do these verses tell us about the Bible?**

Say: **The Bible comes to us straight from God. We can follow its directions and clearly see the way to go in life.**

Human Scrabble

Topic: The Bible

Scripture: Psalm 119:105

Game Overview: Kids will form words out of letters worn on players' shirts.

★ ★ ★ ★ ★

Supplies: Bible, paper, marker, tape

Preparation: Write a letter of the alphabet on separate sheets of paper. Include two of the vowels—"a," "e," "i," "o," and "u."

Randomly give the letters to the kids. Some kids will have two or more letters. Ask kids to tape the letters to the fronts of their shirts.

Say: **We're going to make sense of all the mixed up letters here! I'll call out a word, and you scramble to form that word if you have the letters. If you have more than one letter on your shirt, take off the letters you don't need and hold them.**

One at a time, call out these words and have kids spell them in this human scrabble board: "God," "Jesus," "Holy Spirit," "guidance," "direction," "wisdom," "love," and "supercalifragilisticexpialidocious" (just kidding).

★ ★ ★ ★ ★

At the end of the game, ask the following questions:

• **How did you make sense of the mixed up letters in this game?**

• **How does the Bible help you make sense of life experiences?**

• **How has the Bible affected your life?**

Ask the kids who have the letters to form the word "lamp." Ask a volunteer to read Psalm 119:105; then say: **God's Word is a lamp to our feet and a light to our path. God's Word guides us and helps us make sense of life.**

Leader Tip

Review any Bible lesson you've just taught, and have kids also think of words to spell. Have extra paper on hand should you need an extra consonant or two! Then simply write the letter on a sheet of paper, and give it to someone to hold.

Magnificent Mirror

Topic: The Bible

Scripture: Psalm 119:9-16

Game Overview: Kids will get a chance to use their imaginations in this brain-teaser game as they test their memories of Bible names.

☆ ☆ ☆ ☆ ☆

Supplies: Bibles, mirror, paper, marker, pencils, tape

Preparation: Write these words on the sheet of paper: "Mirror, mirror on the wall—just show me!" Tape the paper to the mirror.

Have kids form pairs or trios, and give each person a sheet of paper and a pencil. Place the mirror before the groups, and instruct kids to work with their teams to write as many names of people in the Bible as possible using the letters on the sign on the mirror. Encourage kids to use their Bibles, and let them know there's a potential for many names. Here are a few of the obvious ones: Jesus, James, John, Lot, Matthew, Miriam, Naomi, Noah, and Thomas.

☆ ☆ ☆ ☆ ☆

After ten minutes, see what names kids have found. Compile the names for a master list. At the end of the game and as time allows, lead a discussion about the people named in the game. Ask all kids to turn to Psalm 119:9-16, and have boys read aloud the odd verses and girls read aloud the even verses. Then ask:

• **What do these verses tell us about the Bible?**

• **How does the Bible reflect God's will and show us how to live?**

Say: **Just as a mirror reflects our image, the Bible reflects God's will for our lives. It includes stories of past saints, and it reflects what happened in their lives. We can read the Bible and live following God's Word.**

Scipmylo

Topic: Change
Scripture: Ecclesiastes 3:1-8
Game Overview: Kids will do Olympic-type events, backward.

☆ ☆ ☆ ☆ ☆

Supplies: Bible, water balloons, flour
Preparation: Set up a course according to the descriptions below.

Say: **Today we're going to talk about change—the kind of thing that sometimes makes us feel upside down. To talk about change, let's first participate in Scipmylo...that's "Olympics" spelled backward!**
Have kids form groups of four and try these silly, backward events:

• Say the alphabet...backward! Time kids' efforts to see who can do it the fastest—or who can do it at all!

• Run a relay race...backward! Using flour, create two lines on the field, twenty yards apart. Have half of the kids line up on one line, with partners lining up across from them on the opposite line. Tell kids on the first line that they must speed-walk backward to their partners on the other line. Kids from one line will speed-walk backward to the second line, and then their partners will speed-walk backward to the first line, relay style. Explain that although they can't turn around while walking, kids can look over their shoulders to see where they're going.

• Walk the line...backward! Place kids at the end of one of your relay lines. See whether they can walk on the line, backward, without looking behind them.

• Toss and catch water balloons...backward! Form pairs and give one partner a water balloon. The person with the balloon will toss it up and back over his or her head—and the partner will attempt to catch it.

> ## Leader Tip
> Have kids throw the balloons high. That gives their partners more time to attempt to catch them, as well as prevents any direct hits to the back of a partner's head!

☆ ☆ ☆ ☆ ☆

At the end of the backward games, gather kids in a circle. Discuss the following questions:

• **What change did you experience in this game?**
• **What changes do you experience in life?**

Read Ecclesiastes 3:1-8; then ask:

• **What does the Bible tell us about change?**
• **How does God help you handle change?**

Say: **One thing's for certain. Change is a part of life. You can expect it! But God is with us every step of the way!**

Have all the backward athletes give each other handshakes—in a different way, like slapping hands then bumping hips with partners!

Balloon Launch

Topic: Change

Scripture: Malachi 3:6a

Game Overview: Kids will direct the landing of their balloons in this "flight of fancy."

☆ ☆ ☆ ☆ ☆

Supplies: Bible, five balloons, dark plastic trash bag, damp all-cotton mop head

Preparation: Inflate and tie off five balloons. Dampen an all-cotton (no metal parts) mop head, and place it in a dark plastic trash bag. Place the bag someplace inconspicuous near your playing area.

Have children sit in a circle. Explain that the goal of the game is to bat a balloon up into the air and to keep it from hitting the floor. Demonstrate how to gently bat a balloon so it floats over the circle—making it easy for other children to bat.

Launch one balloon, get a rhythm going, and then compliment your kids on their great effort. Then toss another balloon into the center of the circle. Add up to five balloons; then surprise kids by tossing the damp mop head into the circle for them to bat about. (This should elicit lots of surprised laughs.)

☆ ☆ ☆ ☆ ☆

At the end of the game, discuss the following questions:

• **How did you feel when I kept adding balloons?**

• **How was this game like when you're busy with lots of things to do?**

• **How did you feel when I changed from tossing balloons to tossing the mop head?**

• **How is that like change in life?**

Ask a volunteer to read aloud Malachi 3:6a; then ask:

• **What does this verse tell us about God?**

Say: **We can expect change in our lives. But the one who doesn't change is God! We can always count on God to help us in life!**

Sandwich Maker

Topic: Change
Scripture: 1 Corinthians 15:51, 58
Game Overview: Kids will try to make sandwiches behind their backs.

☆ ☆ ☆ ☆ ☆

Supplies: Bible, sandwich fixings (such as bread, mayonnaise, mustard, cheese, lettuce, ham, salt, pepper) plastic knives, paper plates, tablecloth, table
Preparation: Cover the table with the tablecloth, and set out the sandwich fixings.

Ask kids to wash their hands before they play this game. Have kids form two teams, and ask a volunteer from each team to stand at the table. Explain that their teams are really hungry, and the team members would each like a sandwich.

Have volunteers begin making sandwiches while their teams shout out things they'd like on them. The volunteers will try to follow the directions. As soon as they've started, shout: **Time to change, volunteer sandwich makers. Face away from the table, and complete the sandwich making with your backs turned.**

Have teams continue to call out directions. When volunteers have finished the sandwiches, have them bring the sandwiches to the front for presentation.

☆ ☆ ☆ ☆ ☆

Allow other kids to try making sandwiches in both manners—facing the ingredients, then turned away. Let everyone make a sandwich to eat; then discuss the following questions:

• **What was it like to make a sandwich as you faced the ingredients?**
• **What was it like when you faced away?**
• **How is this like facing change in life?**

Ask a volunteer to read aloud 1 Corinthians 15:51 and 58; then ask:

• **What do these verses say about change?**

Say: **Change in life can be good or bad, but we trust that God helps us.**

Peanut Packing Pass

Topic: Choices

Scripture: 2 Timothy 2:22

Game Overview: Kids will wear sticky gloves and pass packing peanuts.

✮ ✮ ✮ ✮ ✮

Supplies: Bible, latex rubber gloves, spray adhesive, four large bowls, trash bags, Styrofoam packing peanuts, tarp

Preparation: Place the Styrofoam peanuts in two big bowls. Set out a tarp (if you play inside) or play outside. Set out the other supplies.

Pass out latex gloves, and have each child put on a pair. Have kids form two teams of equal size, and ask each team to form a line. At one end of the line, place a giant bowl of Styrofoam peanuts. At the other end of the line, place a large empty bowl.

Next, go down each row and spray all the gloves with aerosol adhesive until they're sticky. Say: **When I say, "Pass the peanuts," the first person in line should grab packing peanuts from the bowl next to him or her and begin passing the handful of peanuts down the line. First person, keep grabbing handfuls of peanuts and keep passing them down the line. The last person in each row should deposit the packing peanuts in the empty bowl next to him or her. Ready? Pass the peanuts!**

> ### Leader Tip
> Be careful when using the aerosol adhesive. Use adequate ventilation and avoid spraying skin with the adhesive.

✮ ✮ ✮ ✮ ✮

Play the game and listen to the laughter! Have trash bags nearby for easy cleanup. At the end of the game, discuss the following questions:

• **Did you think this game would be easy or hard? Explain.**

• **The adhesive made the packing peanuts hard to get off your hands. How is that like getting stuck in unhealthy habits?**

• **How can God help you choose to avoid unhealthy habits?**

Ask a volunteer to read aloud 2 Timothy 2:22; then say: **Just as it was hard to keep the packing peanuts from sticking to your hands, it can be hard to choose healthy habits. Let's always look to God for help.**

Toe-Tack-Tick

Topic: Choices

Scripture: Proverbs 2:6

Game Overview: Kids will play variations of Tick-Tack-Toe, using kids as markers.

☆ ☆ ☆ ☆ ☆

Supplies: Bible, masking tape

Preparation: Use masking tape to form large Tick-Tack-Toe boards, one per team of six kids. Make the squares 1x1 foot or larger.

Ask kids to form groups of six. Have half of each group choose to be X's, and have the other half be O's. Instead of drawing X's and O's, the kids will be making X's and O's with their bodies. Tell the X's to stand with their arms crisscrossed in front of them. The O's will stand with their arms forming big circles. When kids are familiar with how to stand, invite them to play Tick-Tack-Toe, working with their group members to choose where to play the X's and O's.

Play again, but this time the object is to *not* get three in a row. Have the first player stand in the middle square, giving the other team a slight disadvantage. This takes a little more thinking, but kids will love the challenge.

☆ ☆ ☆ ☆ ☆

At the end of the game, discuss the following questions:

• **How did you choose to move where you did in this game?**

• **How is this like making choices in life?**

Ask a volunteer to read aloud Proverbs 2:6; then ask:

• **Why should we ask God when we need to make choices in life?**

Encourage kids to always ask God for wisdom, and he'll guide the choices they make in life. Then let kids choose whether to play the game again.

Leader Tip

Blindfold all but two children in each group. Instruct these two players to use their teammates as markers as they play the game, gently guiding them into position. Let children take turns directing the game.

Hair Now

Topic: Choices

Scripture: 1 Corinthians 10:12-13

Game Overview: Kids will help a team member grow hair in this game.

☆ ☆ ☆ ☆ ☆

Supplies: Bible, duct tape, bags of puffy cheese-flavored snacks, bowls

Preparation: None needed

Have kids form teams of five to six, and have each team designate one participant to "grow a head of hair." Have players wrap duct tape, sticky side out, around their chosen player's head—it should look like a helmet.

When each team has wrapped its delegate, distribute a bowl of puffy cheese-flavored snacks to each group. Say: **When I say, "Hair now," begin applying cheese snacks to the sticky head, trying to build the fullest head o' hair. No eating the cheese snacks! Think of them as building supplies! Ready? Hair now!**

☆ ☆ ☆ ☆ ☆

After four minutes, call time and see the hair! Kids can take off the "wigs," then discuss the following questions:

• **Were you tempted to eat the cheese snacks as you played this game? Why or why not?**

• **How is that like the temptations to sin that we face?**

Ask a volunteer to read aloud 1 Corinthians 10:12-13; then ask:

• **Who helps us choose to do right?**

Let kids eat the cheese-flavored snacks and celebrate God's guidance when we make choices in life.

Leader Tip

Instead of having kids wrap the tape around their teammates' heads, you could have them wrap duct tape, sticky side out, around wigs or football helmets and wear them for the game.

Keep Together

Topic: Cliques

Scripture: 2 Peter 1:10-11

Game Overview: Kids will work in teams to keep a ball away from others.

☆ ☆ ☆ ☆ ☆

Supplies: Bible, tennis ball, football, pillow, largest ball you can find

Preparation: Collect the supplies.

Help kids form a large circle, and ask two kids to be in the middle. Hand a ball to one of the kids in the circle. Say: **Try to pass the ball without allowing one of the middle kids to intercept it. Middle kids, work together to intercept the ball. If you're successful or if you cause the ball to go outside the circle, have the one who threw the ball join you. Here we go!**

☆ ☆ ☆ ☆ ☆

Continue the game until all or almost all of the kids are in the middle. Repeat the game, starting out with new kids in the middle. Use a different ball such as a tennis ball, football, pillow, or the largest ball you could find. At the end of the game, discuss these questions:

• **What was it like to be on the outside? the inside?**

• **How it that like being on the inside or outside of a group of people?**

Read aloud 2 Peter 1:11; then say: **Let's treat everyone as the body of Christ. One day we'll all be welcomed together to God's eternal kingdom!**

Befriended

Topic: Cliques

Scripture: Mark 1:16-20

Game Overview: Kids will "sticker" others to get them to be part of their group.

☆ ☆ ☆ ☆ ☆

Supplies: Bible, assorted stickers

Preparation: None needed

Help kids form two groups. Place a sticker on the back of each person in the first group. Then give a few people in this group extra stickers, which they should hold in their hands. The other kids in this group should pretend to have stickers in their hands. Tell the second group (those without stickers) that they must try to keep the people in the first group from placing stickers on their backs.

Begin the game, allowing the first group to chase the second group and put stickers on their backs, or pretend to do so.

When the first group has given away all its extra stickers, stop the game. The players from the second group who now have stickers on their backs will become part of the first group.

Repeat the game until everyone has been "stickered" into one group.

☆ ☆ ☆ ☆ ☆

At the end of the game, discuss these questions:

• **What was it like to "sticker" other people into your group?**

• **What was it like to be accepted into a new group?**

• **What's the difference between being in a clique and being in a group of friends?**

Read Mark 1:16-20; then ask:

• **How do you think the disciples felt to be part of a new group?**

Say: **Jesus' disciples learned from him, then they went on to tell more people about Jesus. They didn't just stay in that band of twelve. Let's keep open to more people and welcome everyone so they can know Jesus.**

Bound to Say Hello

Topic: Cliques

Scripture: Romans 3:22-23

Game Overview: Kids will greet and meet new friends in fun, cooperative ways.

☆ ☆ ☆ ☆ ☆

Supplies: Bible, medium-sized rubber bands, index cards, markers

Preparation: None needed

Help kids form trios, and then hand each trio an index card, marker, and three rubber bands. Instruct kids in each trio to face one another and slip the rubber bands over their wrists to join left hands to right hands.

Say: **Let's give a plain old hello a new twist! I'll give you a series of directions for saying hello to the kids in your trio or to other trios. We'll see if you can work together to greet one another in some new ways. Be sure to keep your wrists joined during the entire activity. Ready? Here we go.**

Read the following list of instructions for kids to greet one another. Allow enough time for each trio to accomplish the tasks.

- **Wave to three other trios. Use different hands each time you wave.**
- **Give your partners a pat on the back and introduce yourselves.**
- **Walk to two other trios, and shake hands. Tell everyone your name.**
- **Write, "Glad to meet you!" on your index card. Each member of your trio must sign his or her name to the card. Then give the card to another trio.**
- **Tap your trio members' shoes, and tell one hobby of yours.**

☆ ☆ ☆ ☆ ☆

At the end of the game, let trios take off the rubber bands. Read aloud Romans 3:22-23; then ask:

- **How was this game like or unlike being in cliques?**
- **What's good or bad about cliques?**
- **Who does this verse say we are?**

Say: **There's no difference between us, because we all sin and need Jesus!** Have kids stand in a circle and bind their wrists to their neighbors' wrists, so they form one big, bound circle. **We all are the body of Christ!**

Box Ball

Topic: Communication

Scripture: Colossians 4:6

Game Overview: Kids will communicate as they bop a beach ball into a box.

☆ ☆ ☆ ☆ ☆

Supplies: Bible, beach balls, large boxes (one ball and box for every group of four to six kids)

Preparation: Set out the supplies.

Help kids form groups of four to six. Ask each group of kids to stand around a box and face one another. Give each group a beach ball, and ask the members to take three steps back from the box.

Say: **When I say "communicate," volley the ball to each player, and then volley the ball into the box. A player may hit the ball more than once, but each player around the square must volley at least once before you can bop the ball into the box. Talk to one another so you know what to expect!**

☆ ☆ ☆ ☆ ☆

Play for awhile, then mix up the teams and have kids play again. At the end of the game, discuss the following questions:

• **What did you say to each other as you played the game?**

• **How does clear communication help you in a game? in life?**

Read Colossians 4:6; then ask:

• **According to the Bible, how should we communicate?**

Say: **Always be full of grace and kindness. Share what you know! We can communicate and help one another in games as well as in life!**

Leader Tip

To increase the challenge, have players stand farther from the box, use a smaller ball, or use two balls.

What's That You Say?

Topic: Communication

Scripture: Genesis 11:1-9

Game Overview: Kids will talk in a foreign language and complete a project.

☆ ☆ ☆ ☆ ☆

Supplies: Bible, crayons, tape, paper

Preparation: Gather enough supplies so each trio will have ten crayons, several feet of tape, and three sheets of paper.

Help kids form trios, and then give each trio their supplies: ten crayons, several feet of tape, and three sheets of paper. Say: **In your trios, take a minute to discuss how you'll make the tallest telephone pole with those supplies. I'll drift around to hear what you're planning.**

After about a minute, announce these two rules: **Everyone must participate! Each person may say only one word. The person wearing the most red may say only "booga-booga."** Pause for kids to find that person and for the person to repeat the phrase. **The person to the right of that person may only say "oops."** Pause for kids to repeat the phrase. **And the third person may say only "yowza."** Pause for kids to repeat the phrase.

Give trios four minutes to complete their telephone poles as they use their languages. When time has passed, ask kids to show off their creations.

☆ ☆ ☆ ☆ ☆

At the end of the game, discuss the following question:

• **Was it easy or difficult to build your project? Why?**

Read aloud Genesis 11:1-9; then ask:

• **Why didn't God want these people to work together?** (See verse 4.)

Say: **The people's desire for greatness was way out of line. So God confused their language and kept them from accomplishing their plans. Communication is a gift from God! Let's use it to honor him.**

Switcheroo!

Topic: Communication

Scripture: 1 Corinthians 15:3

Game Overview: Kids will communicate and help each other switch places on masking tape lines.

☆ ☆ ☆ ☆ ☆

Supplies: Bible, masking tape

Preparation: Place two long strips of masking tape parallel to each other, about eight inches apart, and long enough so all kids can stand on them.

Ask kids to find a place on the tape lines, with one foot on each line, and all facing the same direction. Then have them pull a "switcheroo" by lining up according to birthdays—kids with January birthdays on one end and December birthdays on the other end. When kids move, they'll always have to have a foot on at least one line.

Then pull another "switcheroo" by reversing their positions. That is, you want the January and December birthdays to switch places and everyone in between to arrange themselves in sequence again. Kids will need to communicate and help one another move along the line.

☆ ☆ ☆ ☆ ☆

At the end of the game, discuss the following question:

• **How did you communicate with one another in the game?**

Read 1 Corinthians 15:3; then ask:

• **What important message should we communicate to others?**

Say: **Tell everyone that Christ died for our sins. Good news!**

Belly Ball

Topic: Conflict

Scripture: Titus 3:1

Game Overview: Kids will bounce a ball off their bellies, then face a conflict.

☆ ☆ ☆ ☆ ☆

Supplies: Bible, beach ball, masking tape, large empty trash can

Preparation: Using masking tape, create a line on the floor for participants to stand behind. Place a large, empty trash can several feet in front of this line.

H ave kids form two teams. Explain that each player will stand behind the line and try to make a basket in the trash can by bouncing the beach ball off his or her belly. The team with the most baskets will win.

After teams have played the game once, tell kids they'll play again. This time, all the girls will shoot the basket normally while boys will continue bouncing the ball off their stomachs.

☆ ☆ ☆ ☆ ☆

At the end of the game, discuss these questions:

· How did you feel when I told you the girls were allowed to use their hands to make a basket? What did you want to do about it?

· What are conflicts you face in life? How do you handle them?

Read Titus 3:1, and ask:

· The next time you face a conflict, how should you handle it?

Play the game again, and let the boys play normally while the girls have to continue to bounce the ball off their bellies.

Bouncer

Topic: Conflict

Scripture: 2 Corinthians 6:3-13

Game Overview: Kids will bounce various objects around a room.

☆ ☆ ☆ ☆ ☆

Supplies: Bible, chair, basketball, foam ball, beach ball, two balloons

Preparation: Inflate and tie off the balloons, and set out the supplies.

Arrange the group in a single file line. Place a chair about five feet from the first person in line, and hand a basketball to that player.

Tell the person to bounce the ball to the chair, sit on the chair, and say a conflict (like brothers fighting or parents' rules), then bounce the ball back so the next person can go. Ask the others to shout encouraging words such as "You can do it" or "Keep trying." Continue until everyone has bounced the basketball. Repeat the activity with the foam ball, the beach ball, and finally the balloon.

☆ ☆ ☆ ☆ ☆

After the game, discuss these questions:

• **Which relay was easiest? most difficult? Explain.**

• **What conflicts in life are easier to handle? more difficult? Explain.**

• **Who helps you handle conflict?**

Read 2 Corinthians 6:3-13; then discuss:

• **What conflicts did Paul and the early Christians face?**

• **How did they handle conflict?**

Say: **Paul and the early Christians encouraged each other and helped each other face a variety of conflicts. Through it all, they relied on God's strength and love.**

Say a prayer, asking for God's help in dealing with conflicts just as he helped the early Christians.

Phone Book Folly

Topic: Conflict

Scripture: Hebrews 13:6

Game Overview: Kids will individually attempt to tear phone books in half and then discover how they can work together to solve the problem.

★ ★ ★ ★ ★

Supplies: Bible, old phone books

Preparation: None needed

Say: **We're going to have a phone-book-ripping contest.** Hold up a phone book and say: **Let's see who can rip this phone book in two.**

Make phone books available to the kids, and give each child one chance to rip a phone book in half.

After everyone has tried, say: **I guess none of us is strong enough to tear a phone book in half. But I have an idea how to solve this problem.**

Without saying anything, slowly begin tearing the phone book into sections about an eighth of an inch thick. Then hand a section to each child. Say: **Let's solve this problem by tearing this phone book in half together!**

★ ★ ★ ★ ★

When kids have ripped the phone book in half, cheer and celebrate! Then discuss the following questions:

• **How did we work together to solve this problem?**

• **What are some problems or conflicts you might face in life?**

• **How can you work with other people to solve those conflicts?**

Read aloud Hebrews 13:6; then ask:

• **How does God help us with conflict?**

Say: **God gives us wisdom and strength to do his will. God gives us strength to do the things we need to do. Besides that, he gives us one another. Let's work together in doing mighty things for God, too!**

Startled Steps

Topic: Courage

Scripture: Exodus 14:13-14

Game Overview: Kids will be startled along their blindfolded path to courage.

☆ ☆ ☆ ☆ ☆

Supplies: Bible, blindfold

Preparation: Clear a playing area.

Choose one person to be "It." Blindfold this person, and take him or her to one side of the room. Scatter the remaining players around the playing area.

When you give the signal, the blindfolded player will slowly begin to move to the other side of the room. His or her goal is to touch the opposite wall as quickly as possible, while bumping into the fewest people possible along the way.

Remaining players should stand silent and motionless. Whenever the blindfolded person bumps another player, the seeing player must shout "Hey!" Play continues until the blindfolded player has reached the other side of the room.

Ask "It" to give the blindfold to another player, then join the others as potential obstacles. Have participants take turns until everyone has had a chance to cross the room.

☆ ☆ ☆ ☆ ☆

At the end of the game, discuss the following questions:

• **What was it like to be blindfolded and play this game?**

• **How was this game similar to the challenges we face each day?**

Read aloud Exodus 14:13-14; then ask:

• **How can you trust God to give you courage when you need it?**

Play the game again, having a sighted person walk alongside the blindfolded person repeating, "Courage, God will protect you."

Keep the Courage

Topic: Courage

Scripture: Acts 16:16-34

Game Overview: Kids will play a standing version of soccer.

★ ★ ★ ★ ★

Supplies: Bible, soccer ball, two colors of construction paper, four chairs

Preparation: Mix the construction paper and scatter the sheets on the playing area. Make goals by placing two chairs side by side at either end of the field. If you play indoors, use a foam ball or beach ball and tape the sheets of paper in place.

Tell kids that Paul and Silas had courage to work together to pass along the news about Jesus. Paul and Silas were locked in a jail and couldn't go anywhere, yet they still told people about God (Acts 16:16-34)! Tell kids they'll play a game of soccer, but in this game, they must not move—kind of like they're in jail. Tell kids to give one another courage as they work as a team to pass the ball and score a goal. When the ball is passed to a child, that person will stop the ball and say one thing he or she believes about Jesus, such as "Jesus is God's son," "Jesus forgives me," or "Because of Jesus I'll live forever," then that person will pass the ball to someone else.

> ## Leader Tip
> If you have a small group, make your playing area smaller so kids can easily pass and kick the ball—but not so close that they kick one another! Be sure to space the sheets of paper so kids don't need to kick the ball long distances.

Have kids form two teams, and name each team after one of the colors of paper. For example, you might have a blue team and a red team. Have team members stand on their corresponding colors of paper. Say: **During this game, at least one foot must remain planted on the paper at all times. You can't slide or move your paper, but you may pivot on one foot to move the ball.**

Choose one member from each team to be the "rover." Say: **Rovers, you're free to roam outside the field to run after the ball if it rolls away.**

Toss the ball into the playing area and let the game begin. If the ball goes out of bounds, kids may quickly move to a new paper, but they must stop as soon as the ball comes back into play. When a team makes a goal, allow everyone to move to a new paper. If some of the construction paper sheets are torn, have kids throw them away and ask for replacements. Be sure to tape the new sheets of paper to the floor as well.

☆ ☆ ☆ ☆ ☆

At the end of the game, discuss the following questions:

• **What was hard about this game?**

• **Why does it take courage to tell others about Jesus?**

Say: **Paul and Silas were locked in jail, yet they still told people about Jesus. What courage! You just played a game of soccer in which you couldn't move. You still played together as a team and said what you believed about Jesus. What courage! No matter where we are or who we're with, God gives us courage to say what we believe about Jesus!**

Three Squirts and You're Out

Topic: Courage

Scripture: Matthew 5:16

Game Overview: Kids will protect and then carry a candle in a race.

☆ ☆ ☆ ☆ ☆

Supplies: Bible, red construction paper, scissors, squirt guns, bucket of water

Preparation: Be sure kids wear old clothes or clothes that can get damp. Cut six 3x4-inch strips of red construction paper to represent candles. Fill a bucket with water, and then fill small squirt guns for half the kids in your group.

Have kids form two groups: the "squirters" and the "savers." Have the squirters form two lines that face each other, about six feet apart. Give each of the squirters a full squirt gun. Position the savers at the far end of the lines of squirters, and have them choose a person to be the "candleholder." Hand the candleholder a red construction paper candle and tell him or her to hold the candle in the air. Then tell the savers to form a tight circle around the candleholder.

When you say "Courage," have the savers and the candleholder walk between the lines of squirters. The squirters will try to "extinguish" the paper candle by hitting it with water. When they've hit the candle three times, have the squirters shout, "You're out!" Then have groups switch roles.

★ ★ ★ ★ ★

At the end of the game, discuss the following question:

• **What was it like to be a candleholder? a saver?**

Read Matthew 5:16; then ask:

• **What's it mean to "let your light shine"?**
• **What happens in life to "douse" your efforts to let your light shine?**
• **Who helps you let your light shine?**
• **How can you have courage to let your light shine?**

Say: "Letting our light shine" means showing God's love through our words and actions. Sometimes people make fun of us when we let our light shine. Or sometimes we let our busyness get in the way and we don't put God first in our lives. God wants us to have courage to let our light shine no matter what happens in life. God gives us Christian family and friends, like the savers, to encourage us in our faith. God gives us courage to be Christians and let our light shine for him!

Lighthouse

Topic: Faith

Scripture: Proverbs 3:5-6

Game Overview: Kids will try to reach the "lighthouse" before time runs out.

☆ ☆ ☆ ☆ ☆

Supplies: Bible

Preparation: Be ready to darken the room after you've explained the game. Clear the room of any obstacles.

Gather kids to explain the game, and then select a person to be the "lighthouse" for the group. Say: **In a minute, the lighthouse will stand in one place somewhere in the dark room and whisper words from Proverbs 3:5-6 over and over: "Trust in the Lord." You will close your eyes when I tell you to, then walk in the darkness following the voice of the lighthouse. You have three minutes to reach the lighthouse before time runs out, leaving you "treading water." When you've reached the lighthouse, open your eyes, lock arms with the lighthouse, and join in whispering, "Trust in the Lord."**

Take everyone except the lighthouse out of the room. Have the lighthouse take his or her place to stand (farthest from the door works best). Turn off the lights, and let kids enter with their eyes closed. After kids are inside, give a signal to begin. After three minutes, turn on the lights to see who's left "treading water."

☆ ☆ ☆ ☆ ☆

Gather the group in a circle. Ask those who've reached the lighthouse:

• **How did you feel when you reached the lighthouse?**

Ask those who were left "treading water":

• **How did you feel when time ran out?**

Say: **God asks that we trust him, walking in faith until we reach the goal.**

Crazy Carriers

Topic: Faith

Scripture: Matthew 11:28-30

Game Overview: Kids will create carriers to carry friends.

☆ ☆ ☆ ☆ ☆

Supplies: Bible, towels (one per trio)

Preparation: None needed

Have kids form trios, and give each trio a towel. Have trios brainstorm ideas for using the towel to carry a trio member. For example, they could pull a member who's sitting on it; have a member sit on the towel while the other two hold the towel ends and lift it to carry the person; or have two members get side by side on their hands and knees, lay the towel over them like a saddle, and have the third member ride.

When trios have finished brainstorming, have a demonstration time for each idea. Have all trios try the same carrying method and race to a wall and back. Then have them try another carrying method and race to a wall and back, and so on. See which carrying method was the quickest and the easiest to do.

☆ ☆ ☆ ☆ ☆

At the end of the game, discuss the following questions:

• **What was it like to be carried?**

• **Did you have faith that your trio members would carry you and not let you down? Explain.**

Ask a volunteer to read aloud Matthew 11:28; then ask:

• **How does Jesus "carry us" or give us rest when we're tired or worried?**

• **How can we have faith that Jesus will always help us and never let us down?**

Say: **When we're tired or worried, we need to have faith that Jesus will help us and not let us down. We can read the Bible and pray and encourage our friends to always have faith in Jesus.**

Say a prayer, giving worries to Jesus. Then have kids each take a deep, refreshing breath and have faith that Jesus is always with them and never lets them down.

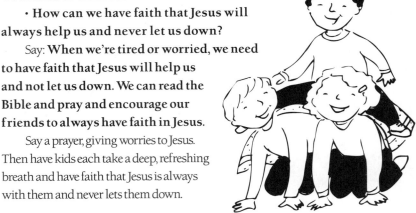

Back-to-Back Instructions

Topic: Family

Scripture: Deuteronomy 32:46-47

Game Overview: Kids will work together back to back as they obey instructions.

☆ ☆ ☆ ☆ ☆

Supplies: Bible, scissors, yarn

Preparation: None needed

Have kids form trios, and give each trio some scissors and yarn. Ask each trio to appoint one person as the "instruction giver." As quickly as possible, instruction givers will tie the other two trio members back to back at their ankles, knees, hips, and shoulders. Ask the instruction givers to tell the pairs to do simple actions such as "Walk five tiny steps in the direction I'm pointing," "Take three jumps in the air," or "Bend side to side ten times."

☆ ☆ ☆ ☆ ☆

Play twice more and switch roles each time. At the end of the game, have kids unwind the yarn, and discuss the following questions:

- **What was it like to work with a partner and follow instructions?**
- **Who gives instructions in your family?**
- **How does your family work together to follow the instructions?**

Ask a volunteer to read Deuteronomy 32:46-47; then discuss:

- **What most important instructions should parents and guardians teach their children?**
- **Why is God's Word so important to follow?**
- **How can you help your family members follow God's Word each day?**

Say: **God's Word is our life! Family members can work together to follow God's Word. Encourage your family to pray together, read Bible stories together, and go to church regularly!**

Rug-Weaving Relay

Topic: Family

Scripture: Ephesians 3:14-16

Game Overview: Kids will make woven rugs to represent families.

☆ ☆ ☆ ☆ ☆

Supplies: Bible, toilet paper, stopwatch

Preparation: None needed

Have kids form groups of four or more. Give each group a roll of toilet paper, and have kids weave a rug with it. To weave the rug, each group will lay out four six-foot rows of tissue. Then kids must weave four six-foot rows over and under the first four rows. Tell groups to weave their rugs tightly so the rugs will be sturdy. Have groups show their rugs when they've finished by gently raising their rugs like banners, holding them in the air, and then walking together around the room once. Time the entire game from the weaving to the walking. Then give kids more toilet paper, and have them try to beat their times as they weave new rugs and again walk around the room.

☆ ☆ ☆ ☆ ☆

Gather all the finished rugs, and have kids sit in a circle around them. Discuss the following questions:

• **How was working with your team like being part of a family?**

• **What can tear apart a family? What makes a family strong?**

Read Ephesians 3:14-16; then close by praying for God's presence and strength for each child's family.

Bumper Buddies

Topic: Forgiveness

Scripture: Colossians 3:13

Game Overview: Inner tubes will cushion kids, and kids will learn about forgiveness.

☆ ☆ ☆ ☆ ☆

Supplies: Bible, four inflated inner tubes or life preservers

Preparation: None needed

Say: **Love and forgiveness help us get along with others. They're kind of like cushions that keeps us from hurting one another. This game will show us what that's like.**

Choose four kids, and give each one an inflated inner tube. Show children how to slip the tubes over their heads and wear the tubes around their elbows. This way, if the tube starts to slip, kids can use their hands to hold it in place.

Help everyone else join hands to form a circle—or boundary—around the "bumper buddies."

When you say "Go," have the bumper buddies walk around the circle, bumping into one another just like bumper cars. After thirty seconds, call time and have each bumper buddy trade places with someone in the circle. Continue until everyone has had a turn to be a bumper buddy.

☆ ☆ ☆ ☆ ☆

Put the tubes away, and discuss the following questions:

• **What kept you from getting hurt?**

• **How were the inner tubes like love and forgiveness?**

Read Colossians 3:13; then say: **Just as the inner tubes cushioned you from being hurt by other people, forgiveness cushions our hearts. Jesus forgives us and helps us forgive others.**

> ## Leader Tip
>
> It's important to keep the boundary circle fairly small so the bumper buddies will bump into one another every time they move. This also prevents kids from running in the circle and knocking others down.

Shape a Square

Topic: Forgiveness

Scripture: Matthew 4:16; 2 Corinthians 4:4

Game Overview: Kids will shape symbols from a rope while blindfolded.

✩ ✩ ✩ ✩ ✩

Supplies: Bible, toilet paper, and three-foot sections of rope (one section per child)

Preparation: None needed

Have kids sit in a circle, and give each child a section of rope. Pass around toilet paper, and show kids how to tear off long enough sections to wrap around their heads and over their eyes several times.

Say: **Now that you're each blindfolded and holding a length of rope, we're ready for our game. Your first goal is to work as a large group and combine your pieces of rope to form one large square on the floor. The square must have four straight sides. Good luck!**

When kids think they have the best square possible, allow them to take off their blindfolds and look at the square they've formed. Try the game again, and this time, while they can see, have kids combine the ropes to form a square.

☆ ☆ ☆ ☆ ☆

At the end of the game, discuss the following question:

• **What was it like to play both versions of the game?**

Have kids close their eyes while you read aloud 2 Corinthians 4:4. Say: **When we sin, we are in darkness and can't see Jesus' light and glory. We stumble through life.**

Have kids open their eyes while you read aloud Matthew 4:16. Say: **Jesus is the light in the darkness. When we say we're sorry for our sins, Jesus forgives us. When we're forgiven, we come from darkness and live in the light of Jesus' love. Jesus forgives us and helps us see how to live each day.**

Have kids remain "sighted" as they use their ropes to shape a cross. Say a prayer of thanksgiving for Jesus' forgiveness.

Multistory Structures

Topic: Friendship
Scripture: Luke 10:25-37
Game Overview: Kids will build multistoried buildings and learn how important support can be.

☆ ☆ ☆ ☆ ☆

Supplies: Bible, index cards, sugar cubes, paper sacks, popped popcorn
Preparation: For each pair of kids, provide a sack of popcorn, a sack containing sugar cubes, and twelve index cards. Be sure to have extra popcorn to munch on later!

Have kids form pairs, and hand each pair a sack of sugar cubes, a sack of popcorn, and twelve index cards. Say: **You'll work with your partner to build two multistoried buildings. For the first building, use six index cards as six floors with layers of popcorn between the floors. I'll time you to see how fast you can build it. For the second building, use six index cards as six floors with layers of sugar cubes between floors. I'll time you to see how fast you can built that, too! Ready? Build your first building with cards and popcorn.**

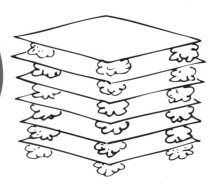
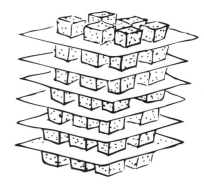

☆ ☆ ☆ ☆ ☆

Time the first building project, and then time the second building project. Gather and admire the structures, and discuss the following questions:
  · **Which buildings were easier to build? Why?**
  · **Which buildings will stand stronger and sturdier? Why?**

Read aloud Luke 10:25-37; then ask:

• **In what ways did the Samaritan support the hurt man?**

Say: **Without supporting our friends, our friendships may tumble.** Have kids blow on their popcorn towers to tumble them. **But when we support our friends with kindness, understanding, and faith, we know our friendships will stand strong!** Have kids gently blow on their sugar cube towers—the towers should remain standing.

Paper-Passin' Pals

Topic: Friendship

Scripture: 1 Corinthians 12:14-20; John 15:15

Game Overview: Kids will put their feet together to discover the fastest way to deliver papers.

★ ★ ★ ★ ☆

Supplies: Bible, paper

Preparation: None needed

Have kids form pairs and sit along a wall at the end of the room, opposite the door. Say: **You and your partner are responsible for delivering your paper to the classroom door, without using your hands. In fact you may use only your feet. Actually, each of you may use only one foot!**

Ask pairs to sit on the floor, close together, side by side, and extend their legs. Give each pair a sheet of paper. Have each partner bend the leg that's not touching his or her partner's leg so that the partners can hold the paper between each other's feet (see illustration). Then partners must figure out how to maneuver themselves across the room to drop the paper at the door.

Leader Tip

You'll see all kinds of contortions as each pair attempts to deliver its paper. You may wish to challenge the group to accomplish the paper deliveries using another method, but continuing to use one foot from each of the partners. For example, all the pairs could line up across the room and the kids could pass their papers conveyor-belt style!

★ ★ ★ ★ ★

After pairs have delivered their papers, discuss the following questions:
- **What did you like about working with your partner in this game?**
- **Why did you need each other?**

Read 1 Corinthians 12:14-20; then ask:
- **What does the Bible say about working together?**
- **Why do friends help each other?**

Read John 15:15; then ask:
- **Who else is our friend?**
- **When has Jesus helped you?**

Say: **Jesus is our best friend. He shows us how to be friends to others.**

Every Body Needs Some Body Sometime

Topic: Gifts

Scripture: 1 Corinthians 12:14-20

Game Overview: Kids will form groups based on information given to them.

☆ ☆ ☆ ☆ ☆

Supplies: Bible, index cards, paper, pens

Preparation: Write either "foot," "hand," "eye," "ear," or "nose" on several index cards. Make a card for each child, and equally divide the cards between the five body parts. Fold the cards in half.

Give each child one of the cards. Instruct kids not to look at them. Say: **Written on your card is one of five body parts. When I say "Go," look at your card and do something that will alert others who have the same word written on their cards. There is, of course, a catch. You can't make noise, and you can't point to the body part. For example, if your card says "nose," you might wiggle your nostrils in and out. When you find a person who has the same body part, stay together and try to find everyone else who has the same word. When you think you've found everyone, sit down. Ready? Go!**

☆ ☆ ☆ ☆ ☆

When groups have formed, hand each group a piece of paper and a pen. Ask the groups to think of three things their assigned body parts do for the whole body. Have each group share its ideas then ask the following question:

• **What happens if one part of your body stops working?**

Say: **Paul says in the New Testament that the church is like our bodies. Each one of us has a special gift. If we don't use our gifts as God made us uniquely able to do, the whole church doesn't work as well.** Read 1 Corinthians 12:14-20 aloud. **Let's remember to use our gifts!**

Wrap It Up!

Topic: Gifts

Scripture: 1 Peter 4:10; James 1:17-18

Game Overview: Kids will wrap each other up and discover gifts from God.

☆ ☆ ☆ ☆ ☆

Supplies: Bible, toilet paper, cotton balls, ribbon, bows, lunch sacks

Preparation: Place toilet paper, cotton balls, ribbon, and bows in five sacks.

Have kids form five groups, and hand each group a lunch sack. Let each group choose a person to be the "gift." The object of the game is for groups to wrap their gifts, using the supplies—and their imaginations! When groups have finished, let them introduce each gift and tell something special about that gift, such as "Our gift likes to help people" or "This gift is friendly to everyone." Allow enough time so all kids can be wrapped and affirmed.

☆ ☆ ☆ ☆ ☆

At the end of the game, gather all the supplies and have kids sit in a circle. Ask a volunteer to read aloud James 1:17-18. Then discuss the following questions:

• **Who gives us gifts?**

• **What gifts has God blessed you with?**

Ask another volunteer to read aloud 1 Peter 4:10; then ask:

• **How could you use your gift to serve others?**

Go around the circle and have kids help each other think of ways to use their gifts at church, at home, at school, or in their neighborhoods.

So Many Things!

Topic: Gifts
Scripture: 1 Peter 4:10-11
Game Overview: Kids will create the longest "liftable" chain.

☆ ☆ ☆ ☆ ☆

Supplies: Bible
Preparation: None needed

Create at least two teams with four or more people. Explain that each team will have five minutes to create the longest chain that can be lifted by its ends without breaking. Instruct teams to use any items on their bodies or in the room and to connect the items in any way they can think of. For example, they can remove jewelry, belts, socks, or shoestrings, and tie them together.

☆ ☆ ☆ ☆ ☆

After five minutes, call time and have each team carry its chain to one area of the room and sit down in a circle. Discuss the following questions:
- **What made your chain strong or weak?**
- **How is your chain of items like a group of people?**

Read 1 Peter: 4:10-11; then ask:
- **What do these verses say about people's gifts?**
- **How are we supposed to use our gifts?**

Work with kids to combine all the chains.

Say: **We've found so many unique items and connected them in a long chain. Just like the items in this chain, God made each one of us unique with special gifts to use to serve him. We work together and use our God-given gifts to tell others about God's love!**

Squirt Gun Volley

Topic: Goals

Scripture: Psalm 16:7-8

Game Overview: Kids will keep their eyes on a target as they squirt balloons.

☆ ☆ ☆ ☆ ☆

Supplies: Bible, balloons, squirt guns (one per child), string

Preparation: Inflate and tie off several balloons. Use string to outline a rectangular area somewhere outside, and divide the area in half.

Have kids form two teams and sit inside the playing area on either side of the divider line (net).

Have teams play volleyball, using a balloon as the ball. Tell kids they must use their squirt guns, not their hands or feet, to push the balloon over the net. Unlike regular volleyball, they're allowed to use an unlimited number of squirts to push the balloon over the line.

☆ ☆ ☆ ☆ ☆

At the end of the game, gather the supplies, and discuss the following questions:

- **What was the goal of this game?**
- **How did you help one another reach that goal?**
- **What goals do you have at school? home?**
- **Who helps you reach those goals?**

Read Psalm 16:7-8; then say: **God instructs us and always goes before us as we aim for goals in life. God helps us and loves us always!**

You're on Target

Topic: Goals

Scripture: Matthew 22:36-37

Game Overview: Kids will take aim at a target and talk about an important goal.

✮ ✮ ✮ ✮ ✩

Supplies: Bible, hula hoop, A-frame stepladder, masking tape, rolled-up socks (one roll per child)

Preparation: Make a target by taping a hula hoop to the top of an A-frame ladder. Create masking tape lines on the floor at seven-, twelve-, and twenty-foot distances from the target.

Set out the sack of socks, and let kids take turns trying to throw the socks through the hula hoop. Encourage and applaud kids for all their efforts. When they've thrown all the socks, have kids gather them for another round.

✮ ✮ ✮ ✮ ✩

At the end of the game, ask the following questions:

• **What was the goal of this game?**

• **How did you feel when you made a goal? missed a goal?**

• **What goals do you have in life?**

Read Matthew 22:36-37; then ask:

• **What should be our number one goal in life?**

Play the game again. As kids make the goals, have them say ways they'll keep God number one in their lives.

Q-Tip Golf

Topic: Goals

Scripture: 2 Corinthians 5:9a

Game Overview: Kids will shoot Q-Tips through straws toward goals.

✫ ✫ ✫ ✫ ✫

Supplies: Bible, straws, cotton swabs, brightly colored paper, various colors of stickers, tape, pencils, "Golf Score Card" handouts (p. 216)

Preparation: Number paper signs "1" through "9," and tape them in various spots around the room or playing area. Make a photocopy of the "Golf Score Card" handout (p. 216) for each child.

To begin, give each child a cotton swab and a straw. Provide stickers, and ask each player to place a sticker on the shaft of his or her swab to identify it.

Next, hand out pencils and scorecards and have kids stand at least six feet from the first sign. Say: **Blow the cotton swab through your straw toward the first sign. If you don't hit the sign on the first try, shoot your swab a second time from the place where it landed. Continue until you've hit the sign, completing the first hole. Then on your score card, record the number of tries it took.**

Play the game as you would miniature golf, alternating turns in an orderly way.

✫ ✫ ✫ ✫ ✫

At the end of the game, discuss the following questions:

• **What was it like for you to aim at the goals in this game?**

• **Did one technique work better than another? Explain.**

• **What goals do you have for school? church?**

Read aloud 2 Corinthians 5:9a; then ask:

• **According to this verse, what should be our goal?**

• **What are ways we can please Jesus?**

Play the game again with small groups aiming at their own targets. As kids aim and shoot, have them tell one another ways they can please Jesus, such as being loving, kind, patient, or telling others about him.

Leader Tip

Be sure to check the size of your straws before the game. Some straws are too small to allow the cotton swabs to pass through easily.

Golf Score Card

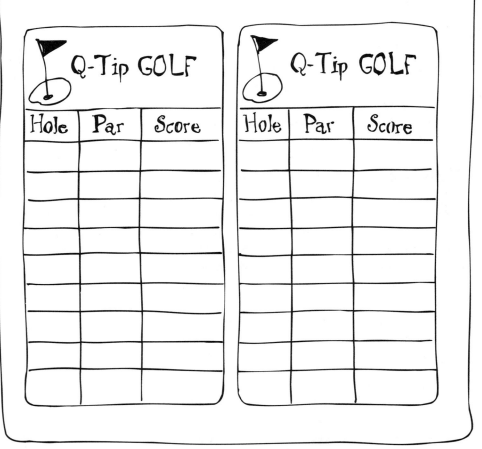

Q-Tip GOLF

Hole	Par	Score

Q-Tip GOLF

Hole	Par	Score

Slap 'n' clap

Topic: God's love

Scripture: John 3:16-17

Game Overview: Kids will experience God's love for them as they receive a running round of standing ovations.

☆ ☆ ☆ ☆ ☆

Supplies: Bible

Preparation: None needed

Have kids stand in a line, all facing one direction. Ask each person to hold out his or her right hand, palm up. Explain that the first person in line will run down the line, slapping the hands of others along the way. When a person's hand has been slapped, that person will start applauding the runner and saying over and over, "God loves [name of runner]." As each person's hand gets slapped, he or she will join the others in applauding and cheering for the runner. When the runner has reached the end of the line, the next person will run.

Continue until everyone has had a chance to run, hear affirmations of God's love, and receive a standing ovation from peers.

☆ ☆ ☆ ☆ ☆

At the end of the game, discuss the following questions:
- **How did you feel during this game?**
- **How do you feel knowing God loves you so much?**

Read aloud John 3:16-17; then ask:
- **What do these verses tell us about God's love?**
- **Who can you tell about God's love today?**

Ask kids to run the race again. Before kids run, have each runner say one thing he or she loves about God. Then have kids run, clap, and affirm God's love for each runner, applauding as before.

Table-Top Football

Topic: God's love

Scripture: Ephesians 3:17b-19

Game Overview: Kids will make table-top footballs and learn about God's awesome love.

☆ ☆ ☆ ☆ ☆

Supplies: Bible, paper, long tables

Preparation: None needed

Give kids each a piece of paper, and instruct kids on how to make table-top footballs:

1. Fold the paper in half lengthwise, and crease it well.
2. Fold the paper in half lengthwise a second time, and crease it.
3. Starting at one end, fold one corner to the side to make a triangle. Keep folding this triangle over until you can tuck the other end of the paper into it.

When kids have folded the footballs, direct them each to take a place along one end of a table and use their fingers to flick their footballs.

★ ★ ★ ★ ★

Encourage kids to try to get the footballs to the other side without the footballs falling off the table. After kids have practiced for a while, have them hold their footballs while you read aloud Ephesians 3:17b-19. Discuss:

• **What do these verses say about God's love?**
• **How do you feel knowing God loves you so much?**

Have kids stand at the end of the long tables and see how long, high, wide, and deep they can flick their footballs.

Say: **God's love is longer, higher, wider, and deeper than anything we can imagine. There's nothing we can do to earn God's awesome gift of love. What a good God!**

Outsmart the Crushers

Topic: Joy

Scripture: John 15:11; James 1:2-4

Game Overview: Kids will sculpt "joy crushers" and name ways to beat them.

☆ ☆ ☆ ☆ ☆

Supplies: Bible, modeling dough, stopwatch

Preparation: None needed

Give each child a lump of modeling dough, and give kids two minutes to shape the lumps into "joy crushers"—something that gets in the way of their happiness—for example, a person (shape a head), an attitude (shape a frown), a circumstance (shape a pencil for homework), and so on.

Call time after two minutes. Ask kids to display and explain their crushers whether they've finished them or not.

Say: **What a lot of joy crushers! Working under time pressure can be a joy crusher, too. Let's see what the Bible says about joy crushers.**

☆ ☆ ☆ ☆ ☆

Read aloud James 1:2-4; then ask:

• **According to the Bible, what should we "consider pure joy"?**

• **How can our troubles make us stronger?**

Read John 15:11; then ask:

• **The next time you're down and joyless, how can you remember Jesus' love for you?**

Ask kids to reshape their joy crushers into actions or attitudes that can restore their joy. Don't time them as they reshape their modeling dough. For example, they can shape smiles or crosses. When everyone has finished, ask kids to display and explain their sculptures. Then discuss:

• **How does your action or attitude honor Jesus?**

• **What tip would you offer to help others find joy?**

Muk

Topic: Joy

Scripture: Ecclesiastes 3:4

Game Overview: Kids will play a game like one played by Eskimo children.

☆ ☆ ☆ ☆ ☆

Supplies: Bible

Preparation: None needed

Ask children to sit in a circle. Read aloud Ecclesiastes 3:4; then ask:

- **What kinds of things make you laugh each day?**
- **Why do we feel joyful when we laugh?**

Say: **Let's take some time for laughter and bringing others joy in a new game. One thing you'll need to know for the game is that the word "muk" means silence.**

Choose one person to stand in the center of the circle. This person will point to someone, and the chosen person must say "muk" and then sit totally still without smiling while the person in the center does whatever he or she can to get the person to laugh. If the person doesn't respond to the antics, the person in the center may choose another child from the circle. This person must respond by saying, "Muk, muk," without laughing, and then remain silent. Then the center person may try to make either of the children laugh.

If no one laughs, the person in the center may choose a third child who will respond by saying, "Muk, muk, muk" and will then fall into a similar silence. Whoever laughs first replaces the person in the center, and play begins again.

Play until everyone has had a chance to be in the center or has been "muk." Tell kids to remember to have a laugh each day and spread Jesus' joy wherever they go!

Mummy Relay

Topic: Joy

Scripture: Psalm 4:7-8

Game Overview: Kids will really roll with laughter during this wrapped-up relay.

☆ ☆ ☆ ☆ ☆

Supplies: Bible, bedsheets (one for every five to six kids)

Preparation: None needed

Form teams of five to six kids. Send half of each team to one side of the playing area and the other half of each team to the opposite side. Ask both halves to face each other. Give one person on each team a bedsheet.

On your cue, have the first person on each team lay down on the sheet and roll up in it (kids will need to grasp the fabric in their fists to keep it together). The person must then roll all the way across the area to his or her teammates on the opposite side. The person wrapped in the sheet must then get untangled and lay the sheet out for the next person.

Continue the game until each person on the team has traveled to the opposite side of the playing area.

☆ ☆ ☆ ☆ ☆

At the end of the game, gather the sheets, and then discuss these questions:

• **What was fun for you in this game?**

• **What other fun things bring you laughter and joy?**

• **Besides playing games together, how do you bring joy to your friends?**

Read aloud Psalm 4:7-8; then say: **God brings us the greatest joy. Let's tell others about God and how much he loves them!**

Duck-Feet Race

HIGH ENERGY

Topic: Kindness

Scripture: Proverbs 11:17a

Game Overview: Kids will put on "duck feet" and run a race.

☆ ☆ ☆ ☆ ☆

Supplies: Bible, 8x14-inch sheets of cardboard, scissors, heavy rubber bands, chairs

Preparation: Set chairs in an oval to form a track. Make duck feet by cutting small one-inch slits in the long sides of the cardboard pieces, running each rubber band around the cardboard, and hooking it through the slits or notches (see illustration). Make one set of duck feet per team of six kids. Bring extra "feet" and rubber bands.

Gather kids and read Proverbs 11:17a. Say: **Since a kind person benefits himself or herself, let's practice a little kindness in a game.** Quickly brainstorm kind words or actions kids can show during game time.

Have kids form teams of up to six kids, and bring them over to the "track." Give each team a set of duck feet. Explain that the first person on each team will attach a pair of duck feet to his or her shoes and run around the track. The next player should quickly put the duck feet on and do the same thing. Encourage kids to shout kind words to spur their ducks on! Have them also show kind actions as they help each other put on and take off the duck feet. **Ready? Go!**

☆ ☆ ☆ ☆ ☆

At the end of the game, gather kids inside the track. Discuss these questions:

• **How were you kind to others in this game?**

• **How were others kind to you?**

Say: **Let's remember to keep saying kind words and showing kind actions. When we are kind, we show God's love to others.**

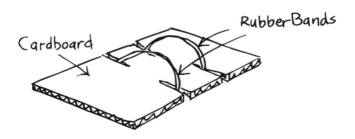

Cardboard

Rubber Bands

Protect Me!

Topic: Kindness

Scripture: Ruth 2:20

Game Overview: Kids will be "workers" trying to get things done while "bodyguards" protect them from paper wads.

☆ ☆ ☆ ☆ ☆

Supplies: Bible, paper

Preparation: Think of some job you need to get done, such as setting up a room for a meeting. Kids will try to do the work in this game.

Have kids form three groups: the "workers," the "bodyguards," and the "throwers." Assign one bodyguard to each worker; and give the paper to the throwers.

Explain a task that you need the workers to accomplish. Say that the throwers will wad up scraps of paper and toss them at the workers, and that the bodyguards will try to bat away the paper wads so the workers can work. Encourage the workers to trust their bodyguards instead of paying attention to the throwers and the paper wads. Each time workers get hit, they have to freeze for ten seconds before they continue their work.

When everyone understands how to play, have throwers begin making and throwing paper wads, and have workers begin working. After about a minute, stop the play and have groups switch roles. Throwers will gather the used paper wads and play again for a minute, then switch roles again.

☆ ☆ ☆ ☆ ☆

After everyone has had a chance to play each role, have kids sit in a circle. Discuss the following questions:

• **What was it like to play each role in this game?**

• **When has someone been unkind to you, as when the throwers were trying to "get you" while you worked?**

• **How has someone showed kindness to you, as the bodyguards did?**

• **When have you showed kindness?**

Briefly tell the story of how Boaz showed kindness to Ruth and Naomi. Read Ruth 2:20; then ask:

• **How can you remember to be kind to your family? your friends?**

Ask everyone to assume the role of the workers, complete the work, and gather the paper balls to put into a recycling bin.

Polar Molar

Topic: Loving others

Scripture: Matthew 24:12

Game Overview: Kids will race to soften frozen gum and blow a bubble.

☆ ☆ ☆ ☆ ☆

Supplies: Bible, bubble gum

Preparation: Twenty-four hours before the game, freeze packages of bubble gum.

Gather kids and read Matthew 24:12. Then say: **Let's play a game to show you what a loveless, cold heart might feel like!**

Give each child a frozen piece of bubble gum. Watch as kids try to soften it up. Say: **When your cold heart gets warm enough, race to blow the first bubble!**

☆ ☆ ☆ ☆ ☆

After kids have blown bubbles, discuss the following questions:

• **How was the cold bubble gum like a cold heart?**

• **What did you have to do to blow a bubble?**

• **How can you show God's warm love to people with cold hearts—** ones who might be sad, lonely, or scared?

Let kids each blow and pop a bubble, then shout, "Burst with God's love!"

cut That Out!

Topic: Loving others

Scripture: John 14:15-24

Game Overview: Create lists of ways to show Jesus' love.

☆ ☆ ☆ ☆ ☆

Supplies: Bible, 13x9-inch pan of rice cereal treats (for each group of five to six children), wax paper, plastic knives, paper, pencils

Preparation: Bake the treats or buy ready-made, individually wrapped Rice Krispies Treats.

Help kids form teams of no more than six, and give each team a pan of rice cereal treats. Give each person a plastic knife and a sheet of wax paper. Tell kids to equally divide their pan of treats and place each section on wax paper. Then have each child cut out a rice cereal treat in the shape of the first letter of his or her name. For example, Kim would cut out the letter K.

Read John 15:14-24; then give each team a sheet of paper and a pencil. Ask kids to work in their teams to create long lists of ways to show Jesus' love to others. The ideas need to begin with the letters of their team members' first names. For example, Kim could say "kiss," or "keep people company if they're lonely." Tell kids they have three minutes to create the longest list.

★ ★ ★ ★ ★

Call time after three minutes, and listen to all the ways to show Jesus' love to others. Encourage kids to add ideas to other teams' lists. Then combine lists for a super long list of loving actions. Have kids munch on the goodies and discuss the following questions:

• **On earth, we're all known by our names. How does Jesus say he'll know us?**

• **Why does Jesus want us to show his love to others?**

Have each child show one other person a sign of Jesus' love that starts with the child's first initial. For example, Tom could "tell" someone, "Jesus' loves you" and Sue could "squeeze" a neighbor in a bear hug.

In a Holy Pickle

Topic: Moses

Scripture: Exodus 2:1-10

Game Overview: Kids will play a variation of Pickle and try to save Moses.

☆ ☆ ☆ ☆ ☆

Supplies: Bible, two sturdy laundry baskets, masking tape, chair

Preparation: For the relay, use masking tape to mark two lines on the floor about twenty feet apart. Place one chair or cone between the two lines.

Have kids form two teams, and place each team behind a line with a laundry basket. Tell one to be Team A and the other Team B. Have each team choose someone to ride in its laundry basket while the rest of the team pulls and pushes the basket. Team A will pull its basket toward the opposite line (making sure to go around the chair or cone). As soon as Team A has nearly completed its circuit around the chair or cone, Team B will drag its laundry basket and passenger after Team A, trying to tag the person in Team A's basket.

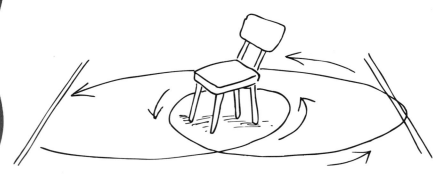

If Team A makes it to the finish line without being tagged, the two teams instantly will switch roles so that those who reached the finish line first now become the chasers and try to tag the other team. The team that *was* chasing will immediately change directions and try to get back to the starting line before being tagged.

If the team that's being chased makes it to the starting line before being tagged, the teams will switch roles and the game will switch directions again. This process will continue until one of the teams has been tagged. Both teams must circle the chair or cone regardless of which direction they're traveling.

★ ★ ★ ★ ★

At the end of the game, discuss the following questions:

· **In this game, what was it like to protect the person in the basket?**
· **How did God protect baby Moses?**
· **How does God protect us?**

Say: **God protected Moses, and God protects us. What a good God!**

Pharaoh's Folly

Topic: Moses

Scripture: Exodus 7–11

Game Overview: Kids will run a wild relay based on the story of the plagues.

✩ ✩ ✩ ✩ ✩

Supplies: Bible, blindfolds (three per team), marshmallows, cups of red Kool-Aid

Preparation: Take precautions to protect the floor from the red Kool-Aid.

Teach kids about the plagues in Exodus 7–11, and then play this wild relay. Form teams of four. At one end of the room, blindfold three members of each team (to illustrate the plague of darkness). The fourth member of each team will stand at the other end of the room. Place some marshmallows and a cup of red Kool-Aid near the child.

On "Go," the blindfolded players will begin leapfrogging (plague of frogs) toward their teammate, who may only "moo" like a cow (plague on livestock) to give directions. Teams might want to work out a code beforehand such as two "moos" means "turn left."

When leapfroggers have reached their teammate, one blindfolded player must find the marshmallows (plague of hail) and red Kool-Aid (plague of blood). He or she will then feed the marshmallows to the second player and give the Kool-Aid to the third player. Have the fourth teammate go to the other end of the room. The three blindfolded teammates will then turn around and leapfrog back to where they began, as the fourth teammate guides them with more "moos."

✩ ✩ ✩ ✩ ✩

At the end of the game, discuss the following questions:

• **What do you remember about the Bible story?**

• **How did the plagues persuade Pharaoh to let the Israelites go?**

Have kids remove their blindfolds and leapfrog around the room some more. Celebrate the freedom the Israelites gained from slavery.

Egyptians and Israelites

Scripture: Exodus 14:5-31

Topic: Moses

Game Overview: Kids will race, tied together, through an obstacle course.

☆ ☆ ☆ ☆ ☆

Supplies: Bible, scissors, heavy string or shoelaces

Preparation: Cut lengths of string long enough for kids to tie around their knees. Create a simple, flat obstacle course in which kids can walk around a chair, under a net, and weave around cones. Play this game in a large gym or outside.

Tell kids the story of how Moses led the Israelites as they fled from Pharaoh's army (Exodus 14:5-31). Form two teams, the Egyptians and the Israelites. Choose one child to play Moses and lead the Israelites, and choose another child to play Pharaoh and lead the army. Describe the obstacle course, and explain that Moses' team will start first, immediately followed by Pharaoh's team. No problem, right? The catch is kids will be tied at the knees with their team.

☆ ☆ ☆ ☆ ☆

Distribute string, and have each team stand in a circle and tie their knees together. Tell kids to say to people on either side of them, "I 'kneed you'!" Then start the race. Encourage leaders to lead! After both teams have finished, have them walk to one area to discuss the following questions:

- **What was it like to work together in this game?**
- **How do you think the Israelites worked together to flee from Pharaoh's army?**
- **How did God help the Israelites? How does God help us?**

Have both teams join together so there's one big mob of kids. Let all of them run the obstacle course together.

Squeeze In!

Topic: Obedience

Scripture: 2 Corinthians 11:16-28

Game Overview: Kids will balance on newspaper and discover that amazing things can happen when they obey Jesus!

☆ ☆ ☆ ☆ ☆

Supplies: Bible, newspaper, stopwatch

Preparation: None needed

Form groups of six, and give a sheet of newspaper (that's the size of a front page) to each group. Explain that the goal is for everyone in each group to stand on the newspaper within fifteen seconds. When kids are on the newspaper, no one may touch the floor outside the newspaper.

If some groups can't figure out a way to successfully complete the challenge, show them how: Each child will stand with one foot on the newspaper while lifting the other foot and holding onto the kids on either side to stay balanced.

☆ ☆ ☆ ☆ ☆

Leader Tip

Double the challenge! Fold the newsprint in half, and play again.

At the end of the game, gather kids and tell them about Paul being put in prison and suffering for Jesus (2 Corinthians 11:16-28). Then ask the following questions:

• **How was being stuck on the newspaper like or unlike being in jail?**

• **Paul obeyed Jesus and still landed in jail. How might obeying Jesus put you in a tough spot with your friends?**

• **What's one way you've obeyed Jesus?**

Do What I Say

Topic: Obedience

Scripture: Acts 5:25-29

Game Overview: Kids will be "talkers" or "listeners" and break some rules.

☆ ☆ ☆ ☆ ☆

Supplies: Bible, strips of fabric, paper

Preparation: For each pair of kids, you'll need four strips of fabric and a paper with the following instructions written on it: "(1) Don't use the word 'I' (eyes). (2) Don't talk with your hands (hands). (3) Don't move your feet (feet). (4) Don't use the word 'God' (mouth)."

Say: **Find a partner. Choose which partner will be the "talker" and which will be the "listener."** Pause while kids do this, then say: **I'll give each listener rules and fabric strips. Don't let your talker see the rules.** Give the listeners the paper with rules written on it.

You listeners need to make sure the talkers don't break the rules as they talk. If your talker breaks one of the rules, use the fabric to bind up the area that's listed on the rules. Talkers, you have three minutes to talk about your faith. Go!

☆ ☆ ☆ ☆ ☆

Allow three minutes. Call time, and then unbind the talkers. If time allows, play again and have partners switch roles. Discuss the following questions:

• **How did you feel during this activity?**

• **How did it feel to have your freedoms taken away?**

• **How did it feel to have your freedom to worship God taken away?**

Read Acts 5:25-29; then say: **Peter had his freedom taken away when he was thrown in jail, but Peter kept talking about God! Always remember to obey God!**

Have all kids take turns "freely" being the talkers and telling one thing they love and appreciate about God.

Kite-Flying Frenzy

Topic: Obedience

Scripture: 1 John 5:3-5

Game Overview: Kids will build their own kites and learn just how important it is to obey instructions.

☆ ☆ ☆ ☆ ☆

Supplies: Bible, heavy-duty plastic trash bags, scissors, transparent tape, $^3/_{16}$-inch dowels, saw, light-gauge wire clothes hangers, kite string, large snap swivels, "Kite Instructions" handout (p. 235).

Preparation: Cut the three to four dowels into fourteen-inch lengths, and make enough photocopies of the "Kite Instructions" handout (p. 235) for half of the group to have one. You'll meet inside to make the kites, and then go outside to try to fly them. The kites will work best on a slightly breezy day.

Form groups of three to four kids. Give each group the materials needed to make a kite. Give only half the groups the "Kite Instructions" handout (p. 235). Tell the other half they must make the kites on their own. When each group has assembled its kite, have groups try to fly their kites. Take note of which groups get their kites to fly most easily (if at all).

☆ ☆ ☆ ☆ ☆

Leader Tip

Instruct groups to work on different sides of the room, so they can't copy each other.

After groups have finished trying to get their kites into the air, gather the groups together and ask the groups who had no instructions the following questions:

• **What was it like for you to try to build a kite?**

• **How did the instructions or lack of instructions affect your kites' ability to fly?**

Say: **Life is kind of like putting the kite together. We can do things based on what we think is right, without directions or guidance, or we can read and obey God's instruction book, the Bible.**

Kite Instructions

1. Begin by taking apart the hanger and forming the wire into a circle.

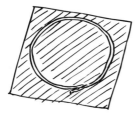

2. Place a trash bag over the wire circle and cut the trash bag around the circle, leaving a one-inch overlap.

3. Fold the trash bag around the back of the wire circle, and tape it onto the wire. Keep the trash bag pulled as tight as possible.

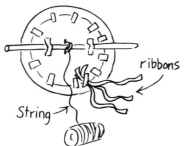

4. Place the dowel across the center line of the back of the kite. Allow equal lengths to extend on either side of the wire circle. Tape the dowel in place.

5. Use cord to tie the swivel to the middle of the dowel (near the center point of the kite). Use tape to help secure the cord and keep it from slipping. Thread the string through the swivel and tie it securely.

6. For the tail, cut four three-inch plastic strips from the trash bag and tape them to the bottom of the kite.

Mosquito Net

Topic: Peer pressure

Scripture: John 11:1-44

Game Overview: Kids will get caught in a net, like mosquitoes, and talk about getting caught in peer pressure.

☆ ☆ ☆ ☆ ☆

Supplies: Bible, rope or masking tape

Preparation: Use rope or masking tape to mark a section about 6x6-feet in the center of your playing area.

Say: **In the jungle, there are so many mosquitoes that people often put a net called "mosquito netting" over their beds or other areas of their homes. In this game, some of you will be "mosquitoes," and some of you will be the "net" that tries to catch the mosquitoes.**

Leader Tip

Modify the size of the playing area to accommodate the number of kids in your group. Keep the playing area narrow enough to prevent mosquitoes from running too far around the net.

Select about one-fourth of your entire group to be the net. Have these kids stand in the center of the area you've marked off in the playing area.

Say: **This area is the net, and all the kids who are now in this area are part of the net. All the rest of you are mosquitoes. The mosquitoes have to run back and forth through the net. While you're in the net area, the net will try to tag you. If you're tagged, you'll stop being a mosquito and become part of the net and try to catch other the mosquitoes. The only place a mosquito can't get tagged is outside of the net area.**

Have all the mosquitoes stand on one side of the net; then have them all run through the net at the same time. See how many get tagged and stay in the net, becoming taggers themselves. Then have mosquitoes run through the net again and again. See how long it takes for everyone to become tangled in the net.

☆ ☆ ☆ ☆ ☆

When all mosquitoes have been caught in the net, gather kids in a circle and ask the following question:

• **What happened when you got caught in the net?**

Say: **We can also get caught in nets in real life. When we hang out with people who like to do wrong things, it's easy for us to start doing wrong things, too.**

Tell the story from John 11:1-44, and then say: **Jesus showed his friends love, and many of his friends then showed love to others. See whether you can get your friends caught up in a net of love by doing good and loving things for them. They might get caught up and start doing the same thing!**

The Power of One

Topic: Peer pressure

Scripture: Romans 12:2

Game Overview: Kids will bounce numbered balls through a hole.

☆ ☆ ☆ ☆ ☆

Supplies: Bible, sheet or blanket, small balls (such as tennis balls), scissors, black marker, name tags

Preparation: In the center of the bedsheet, cut a hole slightly larger than the diameter of the balls. Number the balls, and put corresponding numbers on the name tags. Lay the bedsheet on the floor.

Give each child a ball and a name tag, and have kids gather around the sheet. Say: **In a minute, you'll place the balls on the sheet and we'll begin bouncing them. Imagine the bouncing balls are pressures you face in life to do the wrong thing. When one ball remains on the sheet, we'll see who survived the pressure and we'll all shout, "Good for you! You survived!"**

Have kids place their balls on the sheet. Next, have kids grab the edge of the sheet with both hands and begin pumping the sheet up and down. This action keeps the balls bouncing in the air and allows them to fall through the hole in the sheet, one at a time.

Bounce until one ball remains. Call out the number on the ball, and have that person raise both fists in the air, as in a victory gesture. Have all kids shout, "Good for you! You survived!"

☆ ☆ ☆ ☆ ☆

Play several times, put away the supplies, and then gather the kids in a circle. Read Romans 12:2; then ask the following questions:

• **In what activities should we avoid going along with the crowd?**

• **What should we not do even if our friends want to?**

• **How can we say no and yet still be with our friends?**

Play the game again, and have the remaining person say one way to be a positive influence on friends.

Fly So High

Topic: Prayer

Scripture: Acts 10:4; Revelation 8:4

Game Overview: Kids will work together to keep a tissue in the air.

☆ ☆ ☆ ☆ ☆

Supplies: Bible, tissues (or anything that floats on air)

Preparation: None needed

Form teams of four to six kids. Say: **Listen to a couple of verses that talk about our prayers "going up" to God.** Read aloud Acts 10:4 and Revelation 8:4; then say: **Let's see what upward floating prayers might look like!** Give each team a tissue, and tell kids to work together to get it to touch the ceiling. They can't use their hands; they must make the tissue rise by blowing on it. When a team's tissue touches the ceiling, have all kids rush to give one another hugs.

☆ ☆ ☆ ☆ ☆

At the end of the game, let kids catch their breath and sit in a circle. Discuss the following questions:

• How are the floating tissues like prayer? different?

• How can asking others to join us in prayer help when we have a prayer concern?

Say: **God hears prayers go up to him! God answers when we pray!**

Whole World Prayer

Topic: Prayer

Scripture: John 17:25-26

Game Overview: Kids will mark a map with locations that tell about themselves.

☆ ☆ ☆ ☆ ☆

Supplies: Bible, world map, pins, markers

Preparation: Pin the world map to a wall where kids can reach it easily. Set the markers close by.

Gather children in front of the map. Read aloud John 17:25-26, and tell kids Jesus prayed for the world. Before your kids pray for the world, ask them to each mark the following three spots with their initials:

- where they were born,
- a fun place they've visited, and
- a place they hope to visit someday.

Help kids find locations when they need help. After children have marked their spots, point to each spot and have the child whose initials are on that spot share about the locations he or she has initialed. Then the child who just shared gets to point to another spot and have another child share.

After the game, have kids join hands in a circle in front of the map. Offer a prayer to God, asking his blessings on all those places in the world. Let kids take turns calling out names of places for God's special blessings.

Mime a Prayer

Topic: Prayer

Scripture: Psalm 4:3

Game Overview: Kids will mime and guess actions, and learn about prayer.

✫ ✫ ✫ ✫ ✫

Supplies: Bible

Preparation: Clear a playing area.

Form two teams—Team A and Team B—and have them line up facing each other in the center of the playing area, about four feet apart.

Say: **In this game, each team will take a turn acting out a message for the other team. You'll have to act out a message using no words, but only actions and hand motions.**

When I give a signal, Team A will begin acting out a message while Team B calls out guesses. As soon as anyone on Team A hears anyone on Team B call out the correct message, he or she should turn and run toward "home," which is the wall behind your team. When you see your teammate running for home, run with him or her!

Team B, when you see members of Team A starting to run for home, start chasing them. If you tag any of them before they reach

home, they must join your team. Then we'll line up again and let Team B have a turn at acting.

Have members of Team A huddle together out of earshot of Team B and choose a message. Suggest words having to do with your lesson, such as "the Good Samaritan," "the disciples catching fish," "the Bible."

When members of Team A are ready, have them line up in the center of the playing area, facing Team B, with about four feet of open space between them. Give a signal, and let Team A begin acting out its message. After Team B correctly guesses the message and chases Team A home, have those children who were tagged join Team B. Now have Team B huddle and decide on a message to act out. Repeat the game as often as you like, with the team sizes changing after each round as kids are tagged and switch sides.

☆ ☆ ☆ ☆ ☆

At the end of the game, discuss the following questions:
- **What was hard about acting out your message?**
- **What was hard about trying to guess the message?**
- **What if we had to act out all our prayers to God? What would that be like?**

Read Psalm 4:3; then say: **I'm so glad that we don't have to act out our prayers. Whenever we talk to God, he hears our message loud and clear!**

Swamp Thing

Topic: School pressure

Scripture: Matthew 14:22-33

Game Overview: Kids will play a game and "sink" lower at different times.

✫ ✫ ✫ ✫ ✫

Supplies: Bible, balloons, masking tape

Preparation: Create a "swamp area" by marking off a six-foot circle on the floor with masking tape.

Say: **We face a lot of pressure during a school year. There's the pressure of homework, soccer practice and games, music practice, and other things. We might feel like we're "swamped" with pressure!**

Invite kids to enter the swamp. Toss a balloon into the swamp. Encourage kids to keep the balloon in the marked area and off the ground as they bop it back and forth. The first time the balloon falls into the swamp (on the floor), kids must go deeper into the swamp, by getting on their knees. The next time the balloon touches the floor, have kids sit on their bottoms. The next time the balloon touches the floor, let kids lie on their backs. When the balloon hits the ground again, the game will end.

✫ ✫ ✫ ✫ ✫

Leader Tip

For more excitement, play with more than one balloon. Have kids name pressures they're facing as they bop each balloon.

Play several times, and then gather kids in a circle. Ask the following questions:

• **What was difficult about this game?**

• **What difficult pressures do you face at school?**

• **How do you handle the pressure?**

Read about Peter walking on the water to Jesus (Matthew 14:22-33). Say: **Peter saw the wind and waves, and he got scared. He took his eyes off Jesus and started to sink. When you feel as if you're sinking with pressure, always look to Jesus. Don't take your eyes off him! Jesus always helps.**

Sit-Down Juggling

Topic: School pressure

Scripture: Isaiah 26:3-4

Game Overview: Kids will attempt to juggle socks.

✮ ✮ ✮ ✮ ✮

Supplies: Bible, clean socks (three per child)

Preparation: None needed

Ask children to sit in two lines, facing each other. Give each child three socks to roll up into three balls.

Ask children in the first line to attempt to juggle socks as the second line watches. Then reverse roles. Finally, ask children seated across from each other to attempt to juggle back and forth, keeping as many socks as possible in the air at the same time.

✮ ✮ ✮ ✮ ✮

At the end of the game, collect the socks, and discuss the following questions:

• **What was hard about attempting to juggle?**

• **Do you ever have to "juggle" lots of stuff in school and at home at the same time? Explain.**

• **How do you remember to worship God when you have lots to do?**

Read aloud Isaiah 26:3-4, and tell kids that when we keep focused on God, we feel peace during the pressures. Remind children when there's a worship service at church, and invite them to come!

> ## Leader Tip
> Don't have kids use their own socks—it can embarrass them!

Rubber Band Pull

Topic: School pressure

Scripture: Philippians 4:6-7

Game Overview: Kids will work together to create the stretchiest rubber band you've ever seen!

☆ ☆ ☆ ☆ ☆

Supplies: Bible, rubber bands (lots!), blunt-tipped scissors (one per pair)

Preparation: None needed

Have kids form pairs, and give each pair a handful of rubber bands and a pair of blunt-tipped scissors. Then have pairs line up against one wall of your room.

Say: **The goal of this game is to create a rubber band that will stretch from one end of the room to the other. It's up to you and your partner to figure out how to use the materials I've given you to make the longest, stretchiest rubber band within five minutes. Ready? Go!**

☆ ☆ ☆ ☆ ☆

After five minutes, see how far the rubber bands stretch. Then have pairs think of pressures they face at school and shape their strand like a pressure. For example, they could shape a long pencil (for homework), a round circle (for the face of a teacher), a football or goal post (for sports). Share the symbols. Ask:

• **What fears or pressures do you face at school?**

• **How do you handle the pressure?**

Say: **Sometimes we feel as stretched as our super-stretch rubber bands. The Bible says, "Do not be anxious about anything, but in everything, by prayer and petition, present your requests to God. And the peace of God, which transcends all understanding, will guard your hearts and your minds in Christ Jesus"** (Philippians 4:6-7).

Leader Tip

Combine the rubber bands into one long strand as kids say pressures they want to give to God. Keep the rolled up rubber band line, and use it as boundary lines for future games!

Knock It Off!

Topic: Self-image

Scripture: Philippians 2:1-11

Game Overview: Each child will wear a towel turban and try to keep it on while knocking off others' turbans.

☆ ☆ ☆ ☆ ☆

Supplies: Bible, towels (one per person)

Preparation: None needed

Give each person a towel, and have kids form pairs. Tell them to take turns saying what they like about themselves, then tossing their towels straight up in the air and catching them. For example, one partner could say, "I like that I can play the piano," then toss his towel up and catch it. The partner could say, "I like that I'm kind to my mom," then toss her towel up and catch it.

> ## Leader Tip
> Allow kids to use their hands in the first few rounds but later try a round with no hands.

After kids have shared several things, have them wrap the towels securely around their heads like turbans. Explain that there will be no teams in this game. Everyone should try to knock the turbans off the heads of opponents while protecting the turban on his or her own head. When a person's turban has been knocked off, that person will put it back on while counting to ten, then resume playing.

☆ ☆ ☆ ☆ ☆

Play for several minutes, and then call time and gather the towels. Have kids sit in a circle and discuss the following questions:

• **How did it feel to play this game?**

• **How was knocking off a turban like putting someone down?**

• **How do we keep our self-image high and positive in the midst of putdowns?**

Read Philippians 2:1-11; then ask:

• **How does the Bible say we should treat each other?**

• **What can we learn from Christ's example?**

Have kids pat their partners' backs and say, "You're awesome!"

Who's Behind the Mask?

Topic: Self-image

Scripture: 1 Peter 2:9

Game Overview: Kids will combine their artistic and social skills in this mask-making game.

☆ ☆ ☆ ☆ ☆

Supplies: Bible, paper plates, tape, craft sticks, markers

Preparation: Set out the supplies.

Gather kids around the supplies, and have each person draw a self-portrait on the front of a paper plate. Then show kids how to tape a craft stick to the back of a plate to make a hand-held mask.

Say: **On the back of your mask, list five things you like about yourself. You might list things such as "I'm generous—I like to give people gifts," "I'm very smart at math," "I like to make people laugh," or "I can sing really well." Just don't write your name!**

As kids complete their lists, have them place their masks in a pile on the floor. Have each person choose a mask from the pile and join the circle. Then let each person take a turn holding the mask in front of his or her face and reading aloud the list on the back of the mask. Kids will try to guess whose mask the person is holding.

☆ ☆ ☆ ☆ ☆

At the end of the game, discuss these questions:

• **Was it easy or hard for you to write things you like about yourself? Explain.**

• **Would you have had an easier time if I had you write things you didn't like about yourself? Explain.**

• **Why is it important to have a good, positive self-image?**

Read 1 Peter 2:9; then ask:

• **What does this verse say about who you are?**

Say: **We're chosen by God! We're royalty! Think of that the next time you need a boost to your self-image!**

Hang the masks where kids can see them each time they come to class.

Car-Wash Games

Topic: Service

Scripture: Psalm 100:2

Game Overview: Kids will play various games during a car wash.

☆ ☆ ☆ ☆ ☆

Supplies: Bible, car-wash supplies

Preparation: Tell church members that your group of kids will have a free car wash. Set out the supplies needed for the car wash.

Serve your church by having a free car wash, and have more fun between car arrivals by playing games. Gather kids for a huddle before the first cars arrive. Read aloud Psalm 100:2; then ask:

• **How does this verse tell us to serve?**

Say: **Serve the Lord with gladness! We're going to have fun while we're serving. You'll see what I mean!**

Play these games:

• When a car drives up to get washed, have kids try to correctly guess the make, model, and year of the car.

• When kids see the following cars anywhere in the vicinity, they will respond with the corresponding action:

    1. Volkswagen bug: Shout, "Slug bug!"

    2. Mustang: Shout, "Giddy-up!"

    3. Corvette: Shout, "Va-room!"

    4. Cadillac: Shout, "Pass the Grey Poupon!"

• During a lull, have two teams play this game. One team will line up single file and get a bucket of clean water and a clean sponge. The other team will line up single file, about ten feet away. The first person on the sponge-and-bucket team will throw the sponge at the other team. If the first person on that team is hit, the sponge-and-bucket team gets one point; if the second person is hit, the team gets two points, and so on. Each member of the first team will get a chance to throw the sponge, and then have teams switch roles.

☆ ☆ ☆ ☆ ☆

At the end of the car wash, have kids perform one more service by cleaning up after themselves.

Gather everyone in a circle, and have kids rub one another's shoulders. Congratulate the servants on a job well done!

Garbage Hunt

Topic: Service

Scripture: Genesis 1:28b

Game Overview: Kids will participate in a garbage scavenger hunt.

★ ★ ★ ★ ☆

Supplies: Bible, garbage bags (one per group of four), gloves (one per child)

Preparation: Collect the supplies. Decide whether you'll have the group clean up your church grounds or a nearby park. Get parents to help car pool and chaperone.

Either work at your church, or travel to a nearby park. Have kids form groups of four. Give each group one trash bag and four pairs of gloves. Say: **You have twenty minutes to work with your group to pick up the most trash possible.** State the boundaries of where kids can go. Send adults with kids wherever they go. Tell them to be back in twenty minutes!

☆ ☆ ☆ ☆ ☆

When time is up, gather all the teams back at an appropriate place and ask teams to display the items they've found. Have kids put items that can be recycled in other trash bags, then gather the disposable trash and take it to a trash bin. Read Genesis 1:28b; then ask:

• **What does God say we are to do?**

Have groups stand five feet away from the trash bin, toss in their trash bag, then shout, "Care for creation!"

Congratulate each team for its hard work and for helping to keep your church grounds or park clean.

Leader Tip

If you want kids to form lasting relationships, have them serve together. Overcoming the fear of getting started and working together to help others accelerates unity and friendship as few classroom experiences can.

Get the Word Out

Topic: Sharing faith

Scripture: Matthew 28:19-20

Game Overview: Kids will play a game and think of faraway brothers and sisters who long for God's Word.

☆ ☆ ☆ ☆ ☆

Supplies: Bible, masking tape, ten paper cups

Preparation: Place a strip of masking tape at each end of the playing area. Place another strip of tape in the center of the room and set ten paper cups on it.

Leader Tip

Make a "river" by placing two lines of masking tape about two feet apart for kids to jump over while carrying the Bibles.

Read aloud Matthew 28:19-20; then tell kids they're going to play a game and practice getting God's Word out. Tell kids the paper cups represent Bibles and the lines by the walls are people who want to read the Bibles. Explain that the object of the game is to smuggle the paper-cup Bibles over the lines by the walls.

Form two groups: the "smugglers" and the "guards." Have the guards stand by the tape lines at the ends of the playing area. Have the smugglers stand around the center area. On "Go," smugglers will run to deliver paper cups over the guards' lines. If smugglers are tagged by guards, they must put their cups back. Challenge kids to see whether they can get all the cups over the lines in two minutes.

★ ★ ★ ★ ★

At the end of the game, discuss the following questions:

- **What was it like to play the game?**
- **How is that like or unlike "getting God's Word out" in real life?**
- **What does God want us to tell others about him?**

Have the smugglers and the guards switch roles and play again.

Forward Faith

Topic: Sharing faith

Scripture: Romans 1:13-16

Game Overview: Kids will carry water balloons on pizza boxes on top of their heads and run a race.

★ ★ ★ ★ ★

Supplies: Bible, empty pizza boxes and water balloons (one balloon and box per team of six), masking tape

Preparation: Fill the balloons with water, and collect empty pizza boxes. Use masking tape to make a line ten feet away from one wall.

Have kids form teams of five or six and line up along one wall. Give each team one empty pizza box and one water balloon. Have each team select one person to be the first to hold the box on top of his or her head, then balance the water balloon on top of the box. The object of the game is for a person from each team to walk to the line and back without allowing the water balloon to fall off the box or touching it with any part of the body. The person then will pass the box and balloon to the next person on the team, who must complete the same action. Kids may use their hands to pass the boxes and balloons to the next players.

★ ★ ★ ★ ★

At the end of the game, gather the teams and read aloud Romans 1:13-16. Then discuss the following questions:

- **What was easy or hard about balancing the balloon?**
- **What is easy or hard about sharing our faith with others?**
- **How do we sometimes "drop" opportunities to share our faith?**
- **When we pass our faith on to someone else, how can we support that person?**

Have kids pass a balloon on top of a box around the circle and say one way to pass on their faith.

Save Me!

Topic: Sin and salvation

Scripture: Isaiah 30:15a

Game Overview: Kids will save one another from being bombarded with soft objects.

✰ ✰ ✰ ✰ ✰

Supplies: Bible, flour, bedsheet, and a variety of soft objects (such as Nerf balls, beach balls, balloons)

Preparation: Prepare a playing area outdoors. Sprinkle flour on the ground to mark two parallel lines that are fifteen feet apart. Divide the soft objects so you have an equal number behind each line.

Form two teams, and have one team stand behind each line. Tell kids that when you say "Go," they'll have two minutes to toss their objects at the other team. Tell kids to keep tossing objects so none remain on their side of the line. Call time after two minutes and see which side has the most objects.

Equally divide the objects, and play the game again. Encourage teams to try to get rid of all their objects. Then gather kids, and read aloud Isaiah 30:15a. Ask:

- **What does this verse tell us about salvation?**
- **What does "salvation" mean?**

Say: **Jesus took our sins with him to the cross, suffered, died, and rose again for us. Because of Jesus, we'll live forever—that's salvation!**

Let kids take turns "saving" their teammates from the objects. Ask one team to stand behind one line. Give a bedsheet to two kids on that team, and have the kids unfurl the sheet to use as a shield. Ask their team members to gather behind the sheet. Ask the other team to gather all the soft objects and stand behind the opposite line, fifteen feet away. On "Go," have one team toss their objects while the two kids use the sheet to catch or block the objects and save the others from being hit. Play the game again, and let each team experience salvation from the objects. Play several times, letting different kids hold the sheet.

✰ ✰ ✰ ✰ ✰

At the end of the game, discuss these questions:

- **How did you "save" your teammates from being hit by the objects?**
- **How does Jesus save you from your sins?**

Offer a prayer of thanks for Jesus—our salvation.

Jesus Is the Key

Topic: Sin and salvation

Scripture: John 14:6

Game Overview: Kids will go on a hunt for keys.

✮ ✮ ✮ ✮ ✮

Supplies: Bible, old keys (ask church members to bring keys they no longer use), lock-and-key set

Preparation: Hide the keys throughout the church. (Remember where you've hidden them!) Keep the lock-and-key set with you, with the key in an inconspicuous place that you can easily reach.

Have kids go on a hunt to find the keys you've hidden. Say: **I've hidden lots of keys, and your job is to find them. When you find a key, bring it back, and place it in a pile. When you've found all the keys, we'll try them in the lock. Only one key will open the lock.**

✮ ✮ ✮ ✮ ✮

After kids have returned all the keys and opened the lock, have someone read John 14:6. Ask the following questions:

• **How does the key that opened the lock remind you of Jesus?**
• **How did Jesus make it possible for us to come to God?**

Say: **Because Jesus died for our sins and rose again, we can come to God. Jesus is the resurrection and the life. All who believe in Jesus will live forever with God, too!**

Throw and Stoop

Topic: Teamwork

Scripture: Romans 12:5

Game Overview: Kids will do a combination of throwing, catching, and stooping as they work with their team.

☆ ☆ ☆ ☆ ☆

Supplies: Bible, balls (volleyball sized or bigger)

Preparation: None needed

Form teams of six to eight players, and have team members line up, one behind the other. Pick a leader for each team. Ask leaders to stand four feet in front of their team's line and face their teams.

To start the game, give each leader a ball. Each leader will throw the ball to the first team member, who then will throw the ball back to the leader and stoop in place. The leader then will throw the ball over the stooped player to the next teammate, who will throw the ball back to the leader and stoop in place. If a players drops the ball, that player must retrieve it and return to his or her position before throwing it back.

Leaders will continue to throw to the next team members in line until the last team member has the ball.

The last people then will carry the ball to the front and become the leaders. The previous leaders will take their places at the front of their teams' lines. Repeat the game until the original leaders are the leaders again.

☆　☆　☆　☆　☆

At the end of the game, discuss the following questions:
- **How did you work as a team in this game?**
- **When do you have to work as a team at school? home? church?**

Read aloud Romans 12:5; then have kids play the game again. Each time they toss or catch the ball and until they've finished the game, have kids say again and again one of these words: "body," "of," and "Christ."

Teamwork Pizzeria

Topic: Teamwork

Scripture: Matthew 4:18-22

Game Overview: Kids will love making dessert pizzas at the Teamwork Pizzeria.

☆ ☆ ☆ ☆ ☆

Supplies: Bible, napkins, canned icing, plastic knives, raisins, candied fruits, chocolate chips, raisins, gumdrops, plain sugar cookies (one for each child)

Preparation: Set out the "pizza" ingredients in the following order: cookies, icing, toppings, and napkins.

Gather kids near the ingredients table, and welcome them to the Teamwork Pizzeria.

Form three teams, and number them from one to three. Say: **Team 1, you're the "spreaders." You'll spread icing on the cookie pizzas. Team 2, you'll be the "terrific toppers." You'll add toppings to the mini-pizzas. And Team 3, you'll be the "sweet servers," who'll place the pizzas on napkins and set them at the opposite end of the room to eat later.**

As you work, keep your ears tuned because when I say, "Sweet switch," each person must change to a new job. Ready? Let's go to work!

Be sure to call "Sweet switch" three times. When kids have finished the cookie pizzas, invite them to eat at Teamwork Pizzeria and chat with all team members.

☆ ☆ ☆ ☆ ☆

Help kids get to know one another by asking the following questions:

• **What's your favorite part of school? Why?**

• **What do you like to do on vacation? Why?**

• **If you could be on any team in the world, what would it be? Who'd you like to meet?**

Say: **One of the greatest examples of teamwork was Jesus and the disciples.** Hold up a Bible and read Matthew 4:18-22. **Because of Jesus and the disciples, look at how many team members are here today! Let's always be like Jesus!**

Ask kids to "follow you" and work as a team to clean up.

Leader Tip

If you plan to use gumdrops, you may want to use scissors to snip them into thirds for colorful candy slices.

Um! Good!

Topic: Thankfulness

Scripture: 1 Chronicles 16:8-9

Game Overview: Kids will "eat up" this tasty game as they give thanks.

☆ ☆ ☆ ☆ ☆

Supplies: Bible, plain M&M's, paper plates, cups

Preparation: For each team of six kids, pour an equal number of M&M's into a cup.

Tell kids they get to play a game and give thanks to God in a tasty way. Form teams of six kids, and give each team a cup of plain M&M's and a paper plate. Have the first person on each team dump the cup onto the paper plate and pick up (but not yet eat) only the yellow ones. When finished, he or she will put the remaining M&M's back into the cup and pass it on. The second person will repeat the same process and pick up only the orange ones. Remaining team members will continue to take turns picking up the other colors. When everyone has some M&M's, start the race. For each M&M's candy kids eat, they have to say one thing they're thankful for. As each team finishes its M&M's, have kids encourage other teams as they finish. Kids will give many thanks and eat many M&M's!

☆ ☆ ☆ ☆ ☆

Read aloud 1 Chronicles 16:8-9; then ask:
- **What do these verses say about thanking God?**
- **What "wonderful acts" has God done in your life?**
- **Why should we tell our thanks to God?**

Say: **Our God is so wonderful to us and gives us such good gifts. Let's always remember to give God thanks.**

Marbleous

Topic: Thankfulness

Scripture: 1 Thessalonians 3:12

Game Overview: Kids will catch marbles and give thanks for one another.

☆ ☆ ☆ ☆ ☆

Supplies: Bible, masking tape, box, 100 marbles, paper cups (one per child)

Preparation: None needed

Give each child a cup, and have kids line up on one end of the room. Hold the box of marbles, and stand on the other side of the room.

Read 1 Thessalonians 3:12; and say: **I'm just spilling over with thanks to God for all of you. I have to show you how much I appreciate you!**

Tell kids you'll spill the box of marbles toward them, and they'll have to catch as many as they can, using only their cups—no hands allowed.

Have kids count the marbles in their cups, then help you collect the marbles back into the box.

Play several rounds so kids can try to catch more of the "spillover." Also switch the way kids collect the marbles. For the first round, have kids face you and bend over to catch the marbles. For the second round, have kids face away from you and watch for the marbles by looking between their legs. For the third round, have kids close their eyes and attempt to catch the marbles.

☆ ☆ ☆ ☆ ☆

At the end of the game, have kids come together with their cups of marbles. For each marble in their cup, have kids say one person they're thankful for and why.

Have kids return the marbles to the box as they share.

True-False Tag

Topic: Truthfulness
Scripture: Proverbs 30:8
Game Overview: Kids will take a pop quiz and enjoy it!

☆ ☆ ☆ ☆ ☆

Supplies: Bible, masking tape
Preparation: Use masking tape to make two lines, six feet apart, in the middle of the playing area. Make another line thirty feet behind each of the first lines.

Form two groups. One group will be the "true" group and the other will be the "false" group. Have groups stand on the lines in the middle of the playing area. Have an adult leader, standing a step outside of the playing area, call out a statement such as, "Birds have wings" or "The sky is green." If the statement is true, the true group will run to its line, chased by the false group, which will try to tag the true group. If the statement is false, the false group will run to its line, chased by the true group. Any players who are tagged must sit frozen. The leader will point to them randomly, and they'll call out a different true or false statement.

Try these statements:
• Noah built a house on the sand.
• Adam named the animals.
• The disciples were insurance salesmen.
• Zacchaeus was a very tall man.
• God loves you.

☆ ☆ ☆ ☆ ☆

At the end of the game, discuss the following questions:
• **How did you know whether the statements in the game were true or false?**
• **How do you know whether someone is telling you the truth in real life?**
• **Why do people lie?**
• **Why is it important to tell the truth?**
Say: **God is truth. We are God's people so we tell the truth and flee from falsehood, kind of like the game we've played.**
Read Proverbs 30:8 as a closing.

The Nose Knows

Topic: Truthfulness

Scripture: Psalm 25:4-5

Game Overview: Kids will make a nose like Pinocchio's and learn about truth.

☆ ☆ ☆ ☆ ☆

Supplies: Bible, clay or Silly Putty (handful for each child), mirrors, stopwatch

Preparation: None needed

Set out the mirrors, and give each child a handful of clay. Say: **You have three minutes to use these supplies to give yourself a new nose. When I call time, stop—no matter what your new nose looks like. Ready? Go!** Then let kids go to work molding the clay on their noses to create a new look!

☆ ☆ ☆ ☆ ☆

Call time after three minutes, and let kids model their new noses. Discuss the following questions:

• **What was it like to create new noses for yourselves?**

• **How do these noses create a false front—not the real you?**

• **What are other ways people show a "false image" to others?**

Say: **It can be fun to create new noses as we did. But it's easy to create a false image of ourselves in other ways. God wants us to be honest about who we really are, with others and with ourselves. After all, God made each of us and values us all equally.**

Read Psalm 25:4-5; then say a prayer asking our God of truth to help us be "real" and to always be truthful.

> ## Leader Tip
> Show the clip from *Pinocchio* where his nose grows as he tells lies. Then discuss how lying is another way we present a false self to others.

Hanging on a Tire

Topic: Wisdom

Scripture: Isaiah 11:2

Game Overview: Kids will help one another stay balanced on tires.

☆ ☆ ☆ ☆ ☆

Supplies: Bible, old tires (fifteen-inch work best, one for groups of no more than eight)

Preparation: Tire stores have old tires awaiting recycling that they may loan.

Form groups of eight, and give each group a tire. Say: **You must work together to get all the people in your group on top of your tire at the same time. You can do whatever you want, but no one may touch the ground, walls, or any other support. Once there, I'll ask questions that each team member must answer. Share your wisdom with one another!**

Wait until all the teams have balanced on the tires, and then ask:

- **What's the most important safety tip you have to share?**
- **How would you advise someone to deal with a bully?**
- **What's the number one thing a Christian should remember?**

☆ ☆ ☆ ☆ ☆

At the end of the game, discuss the following questions:

- **What was the hardest part about this game?**
- **How did you help one another stay balanced?**
- **How is sharing wisdom like helping one another stay balanced?**

Read aloud Isaiah 11:2; then say: **Jesus is filled with wisdom. If we need to know anything, we can go to him in prayer. Jesus will help us make wise decisions and lead balanced lives.**

Throwaway

Topic: Wisdom

Scripture: 1 Peter 5:7

Game Overview: Kids will write their concerns and then have a paper fight.

☆ ☆ ☆ ☆ ☆

Supplies: Bible, paper, pencils, trash can

Preparation: Set out the supplies.

Have each child take several sheets of paper. Say: **Write one thing you are concerned about on each sheet of paper. You might write "grades," "family," or "friends." Anything that upsets or discourages you is fair game. Don't put your name on your paper or share it with anyone else. This is strictly between you and God.**

When each person has written at least three to five things, each on a separate page, have kids wad their pages up and form two equal teams. Have the teams face each other, standing on opposite sides of the room.

Say: **When I say "Go," throw all of your concerns onto the other team's side while trying to keep their concerns off your side. The object is to get as many concerns as possible on the other team's side before the time is up. You'll have one minute. Go!**

When the time is up, put a large trash can in the middle of the room and say: **This time, you'll have thirty seconds to work together to get all of the concerns into the trash can. Go!**

☆ ☆ ☆ ☆ ☆

After you call time, ask a volunteer to read 1 Peter 5:7 aloud, and then ask:

• **Was the way you treated your concerns in this game like or unlike the way kids really treat their concerns?**

• **How does God give you wisdom?**

Gather kids around the trash can, and ask for several people to pray that group members will be able to let go of their concerns.

Indexes

Energy Level Index

☆ ☆ ☆ ☆ ☆
MEDIUM ENERGY GAMES
☆ ☆ ☆ ☆ ☆

Preschool, Medium Energy

Early Elementary, Medium Energy

Upper Elementary, Medium Energy

☆ ☆ ☆ ☆ ☆
LOW ENERGY GAMES
☆ ☆ ☆ ☆ ☆

Preschool, Low Energy

Early Elementary, Low Energy

Upper Elementary, Low Energy

Scripture Index